beyond the darkness

{ exposing occultism in america }

SHAWN PATRICK WILLIAMS

Library of Congress Control Number: 2007921795

Edited by: Mrs. Eugenia "Genie" Williams
Graphics & Cover Design: Jeremy Mace www.jeremymace.com

First Printing: March 2007
07 08 09 10 11 12 13   10 9 8 7 6 5 4 3 2 1
Printed in the United States of America.

DEDICATION

Over the past fifty years of American history, our culture has seen a dramatic decline in the Godly heritage in which it was founded upon. The things that are common in our culture today were unheard of for hundreds of years until the past four or five decades.

During these decades of increasing darkness in our culture there have always been a few anointed men of God called to shine the Light of Jesus Christ beyond the darkness. This book is dedicated to all these men who stood up in the midst of darkness and exposed it with the glorious Light of Jesus Christ.

To all the past, present, and future warriors for the kingdom of God, who contend for the truth of the Gospel at all cost, great is your reward.

Gathering the Harvest for the King,
Shawn Patrick Williams

CONTENTS

FOREWORD

During this amazing journey we call life, God allows us the opportunity to meet people that are specially set apart by God. It was during a nine week outpouring of the Holy Spirit that began with one of my "Journey Through Rock" crusades that God allowed me to cross paths with an incredible young man. That young man's name is Shawn Patrick Williams.

Little did I know that God would allow me to pour into an anointed young man's ministry all that the Holy Spirit had taught me throughout a quarter century of ministry. Our "Journey Through Rock" crusades have spanned the world, reaching over three million young people face to face. Hundreds of thousands were saved, healed, and delivered. Literally hundreds more today are themselves pastors, evangelists, music ministers, missionaries, and youth pastors. Shawn Patrick is one of those anointed ministers of the Gospel that I have had the privilege of personally mentoring over the last decade. Shawn Patrick is truly one of the most passionate anointed ministers of the Gospel that I know. He has an unquenchable hunger for God and a burning desire to reach a lost and dying generation with the uncompromising Gospel of Jesus Christ.

Reverend Shawn Patrick is submitted to authority, committed to the call, and totally unashamed of the Gospel.

He is in love with Jesus, his wife and co-laborer in the Gospel, Christy, as well as his two children! I sincerely believe that he is one of God's choice servants and a genuine end-time warrior for the Gospel of Christ.

It is my honor and privilege to call Shawn Patrick Williams my brother, fellow minister, and spiritual son in the Lord. The mantel of ministry is now falling upon this new generation of prophets. Thank you Shawn for continuing my legacy of reaching this generation with the Way, the Truth, and the Life.

Thank you for allowing the "Journey" that God birthed in me over a quarter of a century ago, to continue in even greater power. Thank you for leading an entirely new generation on a journey "Beyond the Darkness" and into the glorious Light of His eternal love!

Reverend William E. "Billy" Mayo

"...YET A LITTLE WHILE IS THE LIGHT
WITH YOU. WALK WHILE YE HAVE
LIGHT, LEST THE DARKNESS COME
UPON YOU: FOR HE THAT WALKETH
IN DARKNESS KNOWETH NOT
WHITHER HE GOETH"
JOHN 12:35.

Chapter 1
BLINDED BY DARKNESS

THE VOW

It was a night I'll never forget! An empty beach with the waves crashing down on the East coast shore; the moon was the only light, however, unusually bright this night. It seemed like I walked for miles without seeing a soul and I was looking. I had just left "The Pier," which is a bar on Jax Beach in Jacksonville, FL. It was my eighteenth birthday. I was alone, on the "streets", drunk, and miles away from what I used to call home. I was angry, scared, hurt, confused, depressed, and deceived, all at once.

It was unusually cold for an August summer night, but then again so was my heart. "God, why have you let this happen to me? Why have you done this to my life? If you are so powerful, why can't you do anything for me? If this is Jesus, I don't want you! Can you hear me God? Are you listening to me?" No thunder, no fireworks, no help, and no God. "That's what I thought, nothing!"

The clouds seemed to move across the sky quickly darkening the light that I once had and then darkness filled my head. Then again, darkness had been filling my head for years, slowly and subtly without notice, gradually bringing me to this place where I now stood. "Satan, if you are real, I call upon you."

That night was the beginning of the worst and most cursed seven years of my life. Over the years, I plunged into drug addiction, greed, paranoia, panic attacks, occultism, sexual bondage, rage, and depression. I was always seeking, but never finding. I was around everyone, but always alone. I had even come to the point of taking my own life. How could I have gotten so far gone, so far away from my Christian upbringing? I mean, I was raised in a Christian family and we went to church several times a week. How could I have gotten so far away from the God of my youth?

PURPOSE

I often ask myself that question. What was it that caused my perception of life and my view of God to become so twisted that I would "sell" my soul to Satan? Was it the compromises that I had made with my choices of music or movies? Was it that one sip or that just one hit that turned into just one more line? Did I barter my soul away in a thousand little compromises long before I actually "sold" it?

Where did it all start? Who or what did it all start with? Was it the people I chose to be around, the places I chose to go, or was it the latest trend I chose to follow? All these questions have surfaced as I have looked back on that night on August 16th, 1991.

Over the years I have met thousands of teenagers that seemed to have been blinded by the same darkness that blinded me and has come to saturate America's culture. Whether from movements, fads, or trends, somehow a whole generation of teenagers has had their minds desensitized and darkened from the light of Jesus Christ, just like I did.

Beyond the Darkness is an attempt to expose darkness in some of the cultural trends and movements by shining the light of Jesus Christ through the Word of God into each topic. Only until we see life through the eyes of God's Word can we truly see what's beyond the darkness.

Chapter 2
UNCOVERING THE HISTORY OF ROCK-N-ROLL

THE INDUSTRY

What is behind some of the Rock Music in our MTV culture in America?

Rock Music is such a huge part of today's culture and has been for decades. I mean think about it, everywhere you go music is heard. When you go shopping at the mall, there is real fast music in most clothing stores. When you go out to eat there is always music playing. Usually, if it is a fast food joint then it is faster and nicer restaurants usually feature slower more mellow music. If you workout, there is always upbeat music playing in the background. Think about every great movie Bad Boys 2, American Pie, and Fast and Furious or video games (BMX video), there is always a "killer" soundtrack to go along with the attraction. And what about all those commercials? The Cadillac commercial with Led Zeppelin! "Oh yeah, Ohhh yeah." Each commercial has a catchy tune behind it that you just can't seem to get out of your head. Look in sports and you'll find music also. The halftime show of the Super Bowl always has a musical number. Even your cell phones and watches have music as a ring tone or alarm. Think about all the musical festivals like Woodstock, The Warped Tour and music channels on TV like MTV, Fuse and BET. You just can't seem to get away from it! I was getting a soda in the mall just recently and after I placed my order they brought me a cup with a lid that had a CD in it by a group called "Simple Plan". You can't get away from it. Music is a huge part of the American culture.

THE GROUPS

The music industry takes in 60 billion dollars a year in revenue and a recent poll taken stated, "The average teenager/young adults listen to 6 hours of some form of music a day."[1] Without a doubt, music impacts our society in many forms through many different avenues. It seems as if entertainers and advertisers have tapped into a powerful and influential vein that has run deep in our country for four or five decades. From the arrival of the Beetles until now there has been a complete musical revolution in America. And it just seems to keep growing and evolving so fast that it is almost impossible to keep up with it.

In the 60's, the Beetles came from England sparking a complete movement in America's youth. The 70's ushered in the "Do what you want to do" attitude with groups like Led Zeppelin and The Grateful Dead. The 80's are known

---

[1] Susan Buttross, MD., <u>American Journal of Public Health</u>, March 2003.

for their Retro style music with groups like The Cure. Nirvana changed the entire music scene in the 90's with "Smells like Teen Spirit" and thus Grunge was born. And in the 2000's, groups like Slip Knot, Audio Slave, Sum 41, and System of the Down have paved the way for this generation of young people.

What are some of the things that all these musicians have in common? What influences have they brought to our society? How is this music affecting our culture? What are the facts about Rock Music? What does the Bible say about Rock Music?

Warning! What you are about to hear will change the way you view music for the rest of your life. Music is really powerful; think about that song that seems to be stuck in your head all day long. You just can't seem to get it out. It seems like it was tattooed in your brain by some unseen force and you can't get it to go away. Or maybe you went to a rock concert and you saw all the people mesmerized by the musicians. Those images and experiences become a permanent part of your memory. I have been to dozens and dozens of music shows and some of the experiences that I've had have left dramatic impressions on my life. I left the 25th Anniversary of Woodstock with a different state of mind. I vividly remember the mudslides, the raves at night, and the seas of people dancing in rhythm. Aristotle once said, "Music controls the masses. Whoever controls the music controls the culture."[2]

With years of experience and a Masters in music, Frank Zappa said, "If one kind of music can make you tap your

---

[2] They Sold Their Souls for Rock-N-Roll, videocassette, Fight The Good Fight Ministries, 2001 (240 min.)

feet, another kind of music can make you double your fist and strike."[3] It is a scientific fact that music affects your behavior. In the "Journal of Personality and Social Behavior," an article said that, "Aggressive music lyrics increase aggressive thoughts and feelings, which might perpetuate aggressive behavior and have long term affects, such as influencing listeners' perceptions of contributing to the development of aggressive personalities."[4] Medically speaking, song lyrics have been proven to shape your view of society and mold your character.

In 1964, four boys from Liverpool, England came to America and radically changed the youth of our nation overnight. They were the best selling group of all time with 163.5 million copies sold with albums like Rubber Soul and Sergeant Peppers Lonely Hearts Band. The "Fab Four", they called themselves, consisted of John Lennon, Ringo Star, Paul McCartney, and George Harrison. But just who were these guys? And what were they all about?

John Lennon said, "Christianity will go, it will vanish away and shrink, I need not argue about that. We are more popular than Jesus Christ now."[5] He also said, "I've sold my soul to the devil."[6] Lennon also said, about his inspiration of two famous songs, "Help", which was written while I was high on pot, and "A Hard Day's Night", "I was

---

[3] Billy Mayo, <u>The Journey Through Rock Collection</u>, audiocassette, SonRise Word Ministries, 1987 (94 min.)

[4] <u>Journal of Personality and Social Psychology</u> July/August 2003.

[5] <u>The San Francisco Chronicle</u> April 13,1996, p.26

[6] Ray Coleman, <u>Lennon: The Definitive Biography</u> (Harper Collins Publishers, Nov. 1992) p.256.

on pills! That's drugs! I've been on pills since I was a musician; I've needed them to survive."[7]

George Harrison said, "When I was younger, with the aftereffects of LSD, that opened something up inside of me. A flood of thoughts came into my head, which lead me to Yogis.[8] Yogis is like Transcendental Meditation, which is a part of occultic practices. Back in the late 60's on through the 70's another English band emerged on the rock scene selling 100.5 million albums. The band? Led Zeppelin. Lead guitarist, Jimmy Page, whose influence shaped all of Led Zeppelin's musical lyrics, was "obsessed with Alester Crowley's (the father of modern Satanism) teachings." Jimmy Page was so influenced by Crowley that he bought his old house in Boleskine, England. Crowley climaxed to major fame in the occult world while living in this mansion he summoned legions of demons there. Jimmy Page wrote a large portion of Led Zeppelin's lyrics in the mansion.[9]

Jimmy owns the largest occultic book store in Europe called, "The Equinox." The Led Zeppelin song "Stairway to Heaven": In 1982, a committee of the California State Assembly convened to listen to the song backward. It said, "He is my prince, sweet Satan, the one who lights up the night, sweet Satan my friend, Satan, He will give you six, six, six." The song played forward sings of one of the top occultic holidays, the May Day Celebration.[10] This group helped start a musical revolution in their time. There are

[7] Billy Mayo, <u>Journey Through Rock Collection</u>.
[8] Ray Coleman, <u>Lennon: The Definitive Biography</u>.
[9] Stephen Davis, <u>Hammer of the Gods: The Led Zeppelin Saga</u> (Boulevard Productions, Jan. 2001) p.9
[10] Billy Mayo, <u>The Journey Through Rock Collection</u>, audiocassette, SonRise Word Ministries, 1987 (94 min.)

still hints of Led Zeppelin, to this day, in a massive Cadillac commercial campaign.

In the early to mid 90's, a band named Nirvana, had a hit song entitled "Smells like Teen Spirit." It changed the course of the music industry forever, thus the "Grunge era," was born. Lead singer, Kurt Cobain, was an open Satan worshipper. On the Never Mind album, Cobain wanted Anthon Levey (the founder of the Church of Satan) to play cello on the album. On 250,000 copies of Never Mind there was a hidden track that talked about going to Hell. Kurt Cobain has been quoted as saying his goal was to "get stoned and worship Satan." Cobain frequently burned song lyrics on church doorsteps and vandalized churches. Cobain's career ended with a self-induced gunshot to his head and a suicide letter addressed to "Bodahh." It was his spirit guide who inspired his lyrics.[11] Nirvana was also known for songs like, "Jesus Don't Want Me for a Sun Beam" and "Lake of Fire," which is a Neil Young remake.

In 2001, System of a Down released an album called Toxicity and in 2003 toured with the Ozzfestivle. Their song "Toxicity" stayed at the top of the charts for months. Off the Toxicity album there is a song called "Soil" that says "You don't realize evil lives inside my mother***** skin, unrealized." On this album they have a satanic pentagram. Also, on the album, System of a Down has a song called, "Chopped Suey." It says, "Father into your hands I commend my spirit, Father into your hands, why have you forsaken me? In your eyes, forsaken me in your heart forsaken." This verse is making a mockery of Jesus

---

[11] <u>They Sold Their Souls for Rock-N-Roll</u>, videocassette, Fight the Good Fight Ministries, 2001 (240 min.)

Christ's death on the cross. Satanists believe that Jesus was defeated on the cross and that He never rose from the grave. Darron Malakian, who writes 90% of all of System of a Down's lyrics was quoted on the thanks section of Toxicity as saying "I thank God, Buddha, Allah, and Lucifer because they're all so lovely and Charles Mansion for his inspiration and honesty." The System of a Downs' lyrics is owned by "Devil Music, Inc."[12] Are these isolated bands or are they a lot more out there? Who are they and what do they believe? Who are some of the bands that are dominating the music industry in this generation?

Slip Knot was described in a Rolling Stone magazine article as "a platinum selling band, famous for tossing feces, drinking urine, lighting each other on fire, and breaking each other's bones."[13] Singer Mick Thompson of Slip Knot said, "Christianity is a ****blight on humanity. There is nothing sicker than organized religion."[14] Corey Taylor started his own t-shirt company called, "Wasted Inc", selling t-shirts that say "I've been denied 3 times, Does that make me a Savior?" and "God is just another know it all ***hole."[15] They have a song called "Liberate" which openly mocks Christianity. They commonly play with the 666 symbol behind them on stage. A slipknot is the knot tied to create a noose. The message is very clear that they are sending to this MTV generation.

Another band that has swept the punk music scene in this millennia is called, "Sum 41." While reading through a

---

[12] System of a Down, <u>System of a Down</u>, compact disc, The American Recording Co, New York, 2000.
[13] <u>Rolling Stone Magazine</u> 20 July 2000:76.
[14] <u>Rolling Stone Magazine</u> 11 October 2001:58.
[15] <u>Rolling Stone Magazine</u> 11 October 2001:58.

skater magazine called "Thrasher," I noticed an advertisement for their album called, "All Killer, No Filler". The bottom of the advertisement said, "Kid tested, Satan approved."[16] In Sum 41's first album "Half Hour of Power" they have song titles such as "Grab the Devil by the Horns," and "Ride the Chariot to the Devil." The band tries to curb the message with mild humor. But listen to their lyrics from their album "Into Deep." The song? "Pain for Pleasure." It goes like this, "The seas have parted the endings started, the sky has turned black. A killing spree through eternity, the devil stabs you in the back." This is a reference to the tribulation period spoken of in the book of Revelation. It goes on to say, "Pain for pleasure, he's the hunter, you're the game, Pain for pleasure, Satan is his name."[17]

TYING IT ALL TOGETHER

Let's take a look at some of the facts. What do all these musicians have in common? The first thing you must understand is they all have ties to witchcraft and Satanism. The second thing is that they all sing about the use of drugs and use drugs. Three of them had very tragic deaths within the bands, John Bonaham, John Lennon, and Kurt Cobain. They all had major impact on the music industry and had or do have very big followings of fans. They all hated Jesus Christ and Christianity.

My mentor is the Evangelist Billy Mayo and back in the late 1980's and early 1990's he held what was known as the "Journey Through Rock" meetings all over the nation.

---

[16] "Ten Years of Templeton" Thrasher Magazine July 2001: Issue 246.
[17] Sum 41, <u>All Killer, No Filler</u>, compact disc, Aquaris Island Records, 2001, Song 13.

He was the man who exposed hidden subliminal messages in rock albums. He has spent 26 years exposing occultism in music.

Back in 2002, my wife and I took up the mantle, and now we hold "Beyond the Darkness" exposés that take you through the past 50 years of Rock and Rap music and expose the satanic groups of these generations.

After telling people this I've had people say, "Is all Rock-n-Roll evil?" Well, it seems that almost every major band that had success in the past 50 years was evil. Does that mean all Rock music is bad? No! But some of you might say, "I really just like the way it sounds. I really don't listen to the lyrics."

THE FALL

God created music for His glory. He chose it to be an avenue to worship Him and connect to Him through the Holy Spirit. Not all music is evil!

In Ezekiel 28:12-18 (KJV), it says, "Son of man, take up a lamentation upon the king of Tyrus, and say unto him, Thus saith the Lord God; Thou sealest up the sum, full of wisdom, and perfect in beauty. Thou hast been in Eden the garden of God; every precious stone was thy covering, the sardius, topaz, and the diamond, the beryl, the onyx, and the jasper, the sapphire, the emerald, and the carbuncle, and the gold: the workmanship of thy tabrets and of thy pipes was prepared in thee in the day that thou wast created. Thou art the anointed cherub that covereth; and I have set thee so: thou wast upon the holy mountain of God; thou hast walked up and down in the midst of the stones of fire. Thou wast perfect in thy ways from the day that thou wast created, till iniquity was found in thee. By the multitude of thy merchandise they have filled the midst of thee with violence, and thou hast sinned: therefore I will cast thee as profane out of the mountain of God: and I will destroy thee, O covering cherub, from the midst of the stones of fire. Thine heart was lifted up because of thy beauty, thou hast corrupted thy wisdom by reason of thy brightness: I will cast thee to the ground, I will lay thee before the kings, that they may behold thee. Thou hast defiled thy sanctuaries by the multitude of thine iniquities, by the iniquity of thy traffick; therefore will I bring forth a fire form the midst of thee, it shall devour thee, and I will bring thee to ashes upon the earth in the sight of all them that behold thee."

This passage tells us that Satan was the cherub over worship in heaven and then fell from heaven because of pride. If Satan led worship in heaven and fell to earth after his rebellion, don't you think Satan had the knowledge to pervert music on earth for his purpose? Perhaps that is one of the reasons music is so deceptive and powerful on the earth in its fallen state.

THE POWER OF SORCERY

Revelation 18:23 says, "And the light of a candle shall shine no more at all in thee; and the voice of the bridegroom and of the bride shall be heard no more at all in thee: for thy merchants were the great men of earth; for by thy sorceries were all nations deceived." All throughout the book of Revelation, it tells us Satan will deceive all the nations of the earth in the last days by the power of SORCERY. The Greek word for "sorcery" is "pharmakeia." It brings about a marriage between drugs, music, and witchcraft.[18] We get our English word pharmacy from the Latin root of this word. Sorcery is the "use of drugs generally accompanied by incantations. An incantation is a set of words spoken or sung in order to cast a spell, very commonly accompanied by instruments."[19] This is very similar to what is spoken of in Revelations 18:21-23.

As these spells are released mixed with music and drugs, demons are summoned and their purpose is to keep the attention of the person under the spell off the activities the spirit was summoned to carry out. In other words, the spells can be sung along with instruments playing and evil spirits will help keep your focus off the incantations or words and on the music. This is the same way Simon the sorcerer deceived the entire city of Samaria in Acts chapter 8. You don't even realize you are under the power of deception, and then the core message of the incantation can work in your life. Our ministry has been preaching this message for years called "Beyond the Darkness", which talks about this in great detail. Visit our website www.warriornations.org for detailed teaching on this subject.

Not all musicians practice this; however, the ones we spoke of previously do. It is not the music's sound that is evil. It is the message coming from the musician. When gauging your music, ask yourself these questions. What are the lyrics saying? What is really behind the message of the music? What message is it giving me? For example, there are a lot of Rock musicians who sing about godly things

---

[18] James Strong, The New Strong's Concordance: Exhaustive Concordance of the Bible (Nashville, TN: Thomas Nelson Publishers, 1990)
[19] W.E. Vine, Vine's Complete Expository Dictionary of Old and New Testament Words (Nashville, TN: Thomas Nelson Publishers, 1996) p.587.

and have a positive message also. Some include: Demon Hunter, Switch foot, Disciple, and many others. Some Christian alternatives on the web include:

ww.soundoflight.com,
www.rochousecafe.org,
tvulive.com.

How do I protect myself from music that is evil? The first step is to have a personal relationship with Jesus Christ. The blood of Jesus is more powerful than any evil. Not only will it wash your sins completely, but also it will protect you from all evil. Secondly, be aware of who you are listening to and what the message is behind the music. When you ask for forgiveness of your sins and ask the Holy Spirit of Jesus Christ to come live in you, He will guide you into all truth. Yes, even in your music.

Chapter 3
THE GOTHIC MOVEMENT

GOTHS

In Beyond the Darkness, we try to cover American movements, arts, and trends that have really had an impact on our culture. The Gothic Movement not only has done that, but it has made international waves, as well.

What are some of the first things you think of when you hear the term "Gothic"? For many people the term "Gothic" is associated with someone who is into things like vampires, death, violence, depression, grave robbing, people involved in Satanism, sado-masochists, people who only wear black trench coats and only listen to Marilyn Manson, or people who paint their fingernails black or maybe someone who is really caught up in the dark side of the music scene. Others might think of "Goth" as someone submerged into a fantasy world or white supremacy or anarchy. No matter what your stereotype definition of a

"Goths" may be, the fact remains that there is a very big sub-culture that embraces the term "Gothic." They range from the "tweens" to adults and they are worldwide! From America to Russia, from Germany to England, and from Canada to Switzerland, you will find them. All different creeds and all different colors, but one thing is common, they all seem to identify and take ownership of this subculture known as the Gothic Movement. As with any movement, there are facts about culture and there are myths.

If you take a trip around the Gothic Web Ring, 640 websites that are totally dedicated to the Gothic Movement, you will find terms like: Weekender/Babybat, Ultra-Goths, Mopey Goth, Perky Goths, and Glam Goths. These are terms created by Goths to describe "Goths." For sure, just like any movement, Goth means different things to each follower. You are classified by how long you have followed the movement. So just what is the Goth Movement about?

Is it a culture of black clad pale-faced band groupies that have a morbid view of life or is there something behind this massive movement called "Gothic" that is driving its followers to the same cause? Our purpose is not to discredit or bash anyone or anything. What I'm striving to do is to investigate the facts without judging anyone. You look at the facts and you decide!

THE HISTORY

Over the years, people who get involved or hear about a topic lose facts behind its origins without ever really knowing its purposes or beginnings. So we want to take a look at the beginning of "Goth". Just what is "Gothic"? Most people think it's only about music. The word

"Gothic" is used in three ways. 1. A building such as a cathedral that is Gothic has a style of architecture that is distinguished by tall pillars; high vaulted ceilings and pointed arches. 2. Gothic is used to describe stories in which strange, mysterious adventures happen in dark and lonely places such as ruins of a castle. 3. Gothic is also a style of printing or writing in which the letters are very ornate.[20]

The word "Gothic" was birthed during the time of the Renaissance (The Middle Ages). It was the name of a German tribe called Visigoth that overthrew the Roman Empire. The term Goth became known as a word that describes an uncivilized or barbaric person. Later in the 12th century it became known to describe a style of architecture in Western Europe. Next it was used to describe a style of horror/ mystery literature that was dark, eerie, and gloomy. Some examples include: Bram Stoker's <u>Dracula</u>, Mary Shelley's <u>Frankenstein</u>, and the works of Edgar Allen Poe. The modern "Gothic Movement" started on the heels of a fading Punk Rock scene. As Punk faded, Goth survived by creating its own sub-culture.

The first use of the term Goth in its present meaning was used on BBC TV. Anthony H. Wilson, manager of a band called "Joy Division", described the band as Goth compared with the mainstream music. The name stuck to bands with that style of music and then the movement began to grow. The movement first became established in London, England in the late 1980's in a night club called "The Batcave." Shortly after that, the Goth Movement hit

---

[20] <u>Webster's Two: New Riverside Desk Dictionary</u> (New York: Houghton Mifflin Company, 1998) p.183.

29

the music scene in California then exploded all over America. Some bands that are considered Gothic include: Bauhaus, Siouxsie and the Banshees, The Sisters of Mercy, Dead Can Dance, The Dead Kennedy's, Skinny Puppey, Morrissey, Forty Five Grave, Depeche Mode. Over the past 15 years the Gothic Movement has taken on an Industrial/Gothic sound with popular bands like Ministry, Nine Inch Nails, Marilyn Manson, and Rammstien fitting in this class. It is impossible to look at the Gothic Movement without understanding that it is all about the music that shapes the culture. We are going to look at some of the bands and the message that is brought forth in their music a little later.

Gordon A. Crews, from the School of Justice Studies at Roger Williams University in Bristol, CT has researched groups he calls the "occult" which –in his opinion- includes the Goth culture. He said "It is up to the individual to define what Goth is for themselves…The mentality is 'I want to be left alone and want to be seen. I want to shock on other people's faces.'"[21] Researcher Jasin Tamlin comments: "If you take a look at the 640 sites that are known as the Gothic Web Ring, you will find many of them filled with desperation, depression, anger, hatred, despair, and angst. A lot of people turn to the Gothic subculture after having a hard time in school, feeling alienated, and looking for a way to express themselves that mirrors those feelings."[22]

---

[21] Wendy M. Fontaine, "Goth Defined: Seminar Sheds Light on what's Behind Mysterious Trend," The Newport Daily News 30 October 2003.
[22] S. Evans & M. Ardill, "Relax, It's Just Black," Toronto Star 25 April 1999: D16-D17.

THE MUSIC

Another important aspect of Gothic is wearing religious symbols as jewelry, which is common. Examples include: the Eye of RA or the Eye of Hours, the Wicca pentacle (a favorite), a satanic inverted pentacle, and the Christian cross. A very large percentage of musicians are associated with the Gothic Movement and do practice some form of witchcraft. Examples are: The Cure, The Dead Kennedy's, Skinny Puppy, Ministry, NIN, Marilyn Manson, Mindless Faith, Magicka, Sabot, Rammstien, and Type O Negative. NIN is one of the industrial Goth bands. Most people do not know what NIN stands for. Nine Inch Nails were the length of the nails used to crucify Jesus Christ on the cross. In a popular magazine, Trent Reznor, the founder of NIN, was quoted as saying, "If you think I worship Satan because of something you see in the closer video, great."[23] On their album, The Fragile, Trent sings, "The clouds will part and the sky cracks open and god himself will reach his f*** arm through, just to push you down, just to hold you down."[24] He was also quoted as saying "Rock-n-Roll should be about rebellion. It should piss your parents off and it should offer some element of taboo, it should be dangerous."[25]

Another Gothic/Industrial group we are going to talk about is Marilyn Manson. Guess who Marilyn Manson was produced by? Trent Reznor! Brian Warner aka Marilyn Manson is a self-proclaimed ordained Reverend in the church of Satan and a recruiter for the church. He was quoted as saying, "Hopefully I'll be remembered as the

---

[23] Trent Reznor, <u>People Magazine</u> 6 February 1995.

[24] Nine Inch Nails, <u>The Fragile</u> compact disc, Interscope Records, 1999.

[25] Trent Reznor, <u>Rolling Stone Magazine</u> 3 March 1997.

person who brought an end to Christianity."[26] He was also quoted as saying, "I don't know if anyone has really understood what we're trying to do here. This isn't just shock value... That's just to lure the people in. Once we've got them, we can give them our message"[27] During his concerts, Manson burns and tears up Bibles and gives altar calls for teens to accept Satan into their hearts and minds. He gets them to chant blasphemies against the Holy Spirit and Jesus Christ. He has also, been quoted as saying, "I think every time people listen to this album maybe God will be destroyed in their heads."[28] Another Gothic band is called Type O Negative. What message is Type O Negative sending to the Gothic culture? Off their album October Rust, on the "I Love You to Death" song they sing, "In her place one hundred candles burning... Black lipstick stains her glass of red wine I am your servant... They say the beast inside of me is going to get ya, get ya, get..." In the song a great description of a satanic ceremony is given. Another song called "Haunted" says, "I'm haunted by her, invades my sleep with tumescent intentions, Hades I'm sure must be missing a demon... Nocturnal mistress, spiral lover...my goddess of the violet, twilight you are lest incarnate."[29] This song is referring to a sexual encounter with a demon spirit. It is very clear the intents and messages of these bands that are being poured into the Gothic culture.

Another Gothic/Industrial band is a group called Ministry. I use to live in Athens, Ga. in an old house on the

---

[26] Brian Warner, <u>Spin Magazine</u> August 1996: p.34.

[27] Brian Warner, <u>Hit Parade Magazine</u> October 1996: p.28.

[28] Brian Warner, <u>HUH Magazine</u> October 1996: p.37.

[29] Type O Negative, <u>October Rust</u>, compact disc, Roadrunner Records Inc., 1996, Song "Haunted."

outskirts of town. One day while high on marijuana, I was listening to a song called "Psalms 69" by this group. All of a sudden I had an urge to spray paint my apartment with graffiti. By the time I was finished spray painting my apartment I stepped back and looked at what I had painted. Without realizing it, I had painted satanic symbols all over my walls and most of the symbols I had no idea what they meant. There is no doubt that these lyrics are dark and blatant with satanic and occultic messages, however, the subconscious affects of the music works deeper than most people realize.

In a CNN report on Anderson Cooper 360 called "Teen Killers" on March 22, 2005, a study was made of all the American high school killers in the past fifteen years. Common themes among all of the killers were liking bands that were considered Gothic or Gothic/Industrial and very dark video games and material. They all seemed to be outcasts hurt by rejection, making a statement.[30]

The #1 largest Pagan, occult, and New Age gathering in the Chicagoland area is called "Ancient Ways." The gathering features lectures by authors of books on understanding witchcraft such as: Full Contact Magick by Kerr Cuhulain and The Journey into Witchcraft by Starsfire Price. The entertainment for the event? It's a local Gothic metal band called "Urn" and "Sacred Gothic Music" by Ragani of the Kirtan. And who is heavily promoting the event? A topical Gothic website on the Gothic Web Ring is the promoter.[31]

---

[30] "Teen Killer," Anderson Cooper 360, television show, Fox News, 22 March 2005.
[31] Fate Magazine November 2004.

No doubt about it, the Gothic Movement is focused on the dark side and it has its roots from dark origins. Not all, but many people involved in the Gothic Movement deal with issues such as depression, cutting, suicide, and drug addiction. So, is the Gothic Movement evil or satanic in itself or is it possible a Goth can be a Christian?

One question I was recently asked was, "I have a lot of friends that are Gothic, they don't really seem bad. Is the Gothic Movement evil or satanic?" The answer- Let's take a closer look at the facts. First, the origin of the name came from a group of people who led an anarchy. Second, everything that is associated with the movement has its roots in darkness. Third, the culture as we know it now started in a bar called the Batcave. Fourth, many Gothic bars cast spells and release incantations on their clubs for success. When I lived in Atlanta, Ga., I personally knew that witchcraft was used over bar businesses, one of which was Gothic. When I moved out of the state to open my own bar, these same gothic people cast spells and released incantations over my bar. The majority of musicians that associate themselves with the Gothic Movement openly talk or sing about involvement in some form of witchcraft. Fifth, a lot of the research done shows a very large percentage of people involved in the Gothic Movement battle major issues such as suicide, depression, cutting, etc. that are very evil issues. Six, there seems to be a common theme in the movement to accept all religions as okay and the movement does support a lot of biblically called "evil" things, such as this event talked about in Chicago. Seven, the fact is that many Satanists and people involved in the occult use the Gothic culture to recruit new members, mostly young impressionable teenagers. When I lived in Atlanta I knew these same Gothic people in the occult who would target young street kids with nowhere else to turn and who were going to these Gothic clubs.

NOT AN OPINION, THE WORD OF GOD

So let's take a look at the Word of God and see what it says about the movement. I do not want to give you just an opinion. I want to look at the truth of the scriptures to make an assessment. In 2 Corinthians 6:14 it says, "Be ye not unequally yoked together with unbelievers: for what fellowship hath righteousness with unrighteousness? And what communion hath light with darkness?"[32] The Greek interpretation of "communion" here is "social intercourse."[33] This scripture clearly tells believers of Christ not to have social intimacy with people who are involved in any forms of darkness or involved in occultism and that would include a movement as well. Remember the question I was asked, "Is it possible for a Goth to be a Christian?" The answer is in I John 1:5-7 and it says, "God is light, and in him is no darkness at all. If we say that we have fellowship with him, and walk in darkness we lie, and do not the truth: But if we walk in the light, as he is in the light, we have fellowship one with another and the blood of Jesus Christ his Son cleanseth us from all sin."[34]

The Scripture makes it very clear that the believer is supposed to follow after the light of Jesus Christ, not a movement full of darkness. I do believe there are Christians

---

[32] Charles Caldwell Ryrie, The Ryrie Study Bible KJV, (Chicago, Illinois: Moody Bible Press, 1978) 2 Corinthians 6:14.
[33] W.E. Vines, Vine's Complete Expository Dictionary of Old and New Testament Words (Nashville, TN: Thomas Nelson Inc.,1996) p.114.
[34] Ryrie, p.1771.

that are involved in the Gothic Movement, but I believe they are putting themselves in a very dangerous situation spiritually because of the atmosphere that comes with the Gothic Movement. Whether it is Goth, metal, punk, or rave, is the movement taking you closer or away from your relationship with Jesus Christ?

There are Christians that are called to minister to people involved in the evil side of the Gothic Movement, but these people lead you into the light of Jesus Christ. One of these people was asked, "How do I become a Goth?" This person answered, "The real question that should be asked is not 'How do I become a Goth, but how do I become a Christian?'"

No matter what kind of movement or group you are involved in the real question is, "How do I become a Christian? "That if thou shalt confess with thy mouth the Lord Jesus, and shalt believe in thine heart that God hath raised him from the dead, thou shalt be saved" Romans 10:9.[35] If you want to receive Jesus as your Lord and Savior, pray this prayer with me. Dear God, please forgive me for all my sin, especially occultic ties of any kind. I repent through the blood of Jesus and renounce all involvement with satanic things. I receive Jesus Christ as my Lord and Savoir and ask the Holy Spirit to come live in my heart. In Jesus name, amen."

---

[35] Ryrie, p.1609.

Chapter 4
BEYOND THE PHENOMENON OF FANTASY BOOKS

THE HISTORY

You may have one yourself or have seen one in a store. You may have wondered, "What exactly is a fantasy book? What are they about? Where did fantasy come from? Who do they reach and how can fantasy books affect your life?"

Well, let's start with, "What exactly is a fantasy book?" "America's book industry in 2003 was $27 billion dollars for the overall year. Children's fantasy makes up 2.5 billion of that figure, which is a huge percent of the overall book market just a little shy of 10%. More than 100,000 books were published in 2003 and over 190,000 in 2004. About 10,000 children's fantasy titles a year aimed at 9 to 13 year olds."[36]

---

[36] "Book Sales Plunge," <u>CBS Evening News</u>, CBS, New York, 13 May 2004.

In literature, fantasy is a form of fiction, usually novels or short stories. Fantasy fiction covers an immense number of works embraced by the mainstream book industry, like Harry Potter or <u>Lord of the Rings</u>, just to mention two of the most popular.

Two different forms of fantasy fiction are called "sword and sorcery" and "high fantasy." These two closely related forms of fantasy typically describe tales featuring magic, brave knights or characters, and/or quests. They are usually set in a world inhabited by mythical creatures, such as dragons, etc. Examples of such books include: <u>The Scorpion</u> by Stephen D. Sullivan, <u>The Lord of the Rings</u> by J.R.R. Tolkien, and <u>Harry Potter</u> by J.K. Rowling. Fantasy themed books have been around as long as Roman and Greek mythology has, but in the mid-20th Century fantasy experienced a big "renewal" with works like <u>The Chronicles of Narnia</u> by C.S. Lewis and <u>The Hobbit</u> by J.R.R. Tolkien.

In the past few decades numerous books, board games, and video games have emerged with the fantasy concepts. Some video games have been recreated as a "fantasy role playing" games such as "Magic the Gathering," "The Forgotten Realms," "Final Fantasy," and "Battletech," which have exploded on the market.

FANTASY BOOKS AND THEIR AUTHORS

It is impossible to talk about fantasy books without talking about the phenomenon that the Harry Potter series has become. In 2001, Harry Potter hit the 100 million worldwide sales markets in only three years. The release of the latest Potter book sold over 2 million copies the first day. Christopher Little, J.K. Rowling's agent was quoted as saying "This is an unprecedented publishing achievement anywhere in the world- either for adult or children's books. Every time we publish a new Harry Potter book, the first goes back up to the top of the bestseller list."[37]

Public school systems have even incorporated Harry Potter into their history, geography, science, and English lessons, hoping to enhance the interest of their students. Beecham Publishing's Exploring Harry Potter, written by Elizabeth Schafer, Ph.D. was designed for teachers with concepts of the application of these incorporations.[38] But just how is this fantasy phenomenon affecting our culture and who are some of the people writing society's most popular fantasy book?

J.R.R. Tolkien, author of The Lord of the Rings was a Catholic, but his influences and ideologies were far from Catholic. Tolkien was quoted as saying, "Reincarnation may be bad theology (that surely, rather than metaphysics) as applied to Humanity. But I do not see how even in the primary world any theologian or philosopher, unless very much better informed about the relation of spirit and body than I believe anyone to be, could deny the possibility of reincarnation as a mode of existence, prescribed for certain kinds of rational incarnate creatures."[39] Simply stated, regardless of theology, reincarnation makes sense to believe in and that is why he used it in his books. He was completely aware of the concepts being consumed through his fantasy books.

---

[37] Martha Kleder, "Harry Potter: Seduction of the Occult," Family Voice, Nov/Dec 2001, p.1.

[38] Kleder, p.2

[39] Kleder, p.2

J.K. Rowling, a former UK English teacher and the author of Harry Potter, majored in Mythology at Exeter University in England. She researched the occult in order to present an accurate representation in her books.[40] She purposely studied the occult to make sure accurate concepts were being given through her work.

It seems very clear that these authors knew what they were writing and did it without hesitation. Harry Potter's author seems to have written the series just to teach occultic concepts to our youth. These are just two authors of the most popular fantasy books of this decade. What kind of impact are these fantasy books having on our culture, if any at all?

I've spent seven years around teenagers who read fantasy books and many of them would become obsessed with these books. Some were a little more consumed than others, but without a doubt, I personally could see the change in behaviors while reading certain fantasy books. It was incredible.

I've found other incidents that affirm a link to the Potter books and witchcraft. In Klagenfurt, Austria there is a school for witches and warlocks. In an article about the school in USA Today it said, "The founders freely thank Harry Potter for the surge in attendance. 'Before the movie came out last year, we had 40 students. Now, we have more than double that.'"[41] That is over a 100% increase in enrollment. Since this release America seems to have had an occultic revival spoken of in the book of Revelation.

---

[40] Kleder, p.3.
[41] Donna Freydikin, "Consider the Sorcery," <u>USA Today</u>, 14 November 2002: 2C.

In Port Coquitlam, British Columbia, a six year old child who refused to read the Harry Potter book because of her faith was sent to the school office for an entire year during the classroom's reading time.[43] Judith Krug, head of the Office of Intellectual Freedom and affiliated with the American Library Association was quoted as saying, "The challenges we have had to Harry Potter have been in schools, which means the children are going to be deprived of what appears to be the biggest phenomenon children's publishing has ever known."[44]

My question is what exactly is the core message behind these fantasy book phenomena? And can they really affect you spiritually or are these examples just isolated examples? You might say, "I know the plots to a lot of fantasy books have central themes of good fighting evil, but it is just a book. What can it hurt to read a fantasy fiction story? Can it really affect my spiritual life? I mean they seem like harmless stories!"

Before I answer that, let's take a look at what is the central core message of the story. Let's take a look at the core teachings. In the Harry Potter and the Sorcerer's Stone there is a chapter called, "The Potions Master." The setting is between Professor Snape and Harry Potter who weren't getting along. It reads like this, "Potions lessons took place down in the dungeons. It was colder here than up in the main castle, and would have been quite creepy enough, without the pickled animals floating in glass jars all around the walls... You are here to learn the subtle science and exact art of potion making," he began. He spoke in barely

---

[43] Kleder, p.1
[44] Kleder, p.4

more than a whisper, but they caught every word- like Professor McGonagall, Snape had the gift of keeping a class silent without effort. 'As there is little foolish wand-waving here, many of you will hardly believe this is magic. I don't expect you will really understand the beauty of the softly simmering cauldron with its shimmering fumes, the delicate power of liquids that creep through human veins, bewitching the mind, ensnaring the senses... I can teach you how to bottle fame, brew glory, even stopper death- if you aren't as big bunch of dunderheads as I usually have to teach'... "Potter!' said Snape suddenly. 'What would I get if I added powdered root of asphodel to an infusion of wormwood?' Powdered root of what to an infusion of what? 'I don't know sir,' said Harry... 'What's the difference, Potter, between, monkshood and wolfs bane?' 'I don't know, said Harry quietly... 'For your information, Potter, asphodel and wormwood make a sleeping potion so powerful it is known as the Draught of Living Death. A bezoar is a stone taken from the stomach of a goat and it will save you from most poisons. As for monkshood and wolfs bane, they are the same plant, which also goes by the name of aconite...''[45]

The Harry Potter series have teachings such as reincarnation, communing with the dead and the spirit world, sorcery, divination, spells, curses, evolution, meditation, occult symbology, black magic, demon possession, and many more aspects of witchcraft. All these concepts are labeled as "abominations" in the Bible and are directly taught to children in these books.

---

[45] J.K. Rowling, <u>Harry Potter and the Sorcerer's Stone</u> (Scholastic Inc., 1999) p.138.

The Lord of the Rings has central themes of reincarnation, physic powers, and a deep Pagan view of thinking. Listen to this short discourse. This is from The Lord of the Rings: The Fellowship of the Ring. "Suddenly a song began: a cold murmur, rising and falling. The voice seemed far away and immeasurably dreary, sometimes high in the air and thin, sometimes like a low moan from the ground. Out of the formless stream of sad but horrible sounds, strings of words would now and again shape themselves; grim, hard, cold words, heartless and miserable. The night was railing against the morning of which it was bereaved, and the cold was cursing the warmth for which it hungered. Frodo was chilled to the marrow. After a while the song became clearer, and with dread in his heart he perceived that it had changed into an incantation: 'Cold be hand and heat and bone, and cold be sleep under stone: never more to wake on the stony bed, never, till the sun fails and the moon are dead. In the black wind the stars shall die, and still on gold here let them lie, till the dark lord lifts his hand over dead sea and withered land.' He heard behind his head a creaking and scraping sound. Raising himself on one arm he looked, and saw now in the pale light that they were in a kind of passage, which behind them turned a corner. Round the corner, a long arm was groping, walking on its fingers towards Sam, who was lying nearest, and towards the hilt of the sword that lay upon him. At first, Frodo felt as if he had indeed been turned into stone by the incantation."[46]

---

[46] J.R.R. Tolkien, The Lord of the Rings-Part One: The Fellowship of the Ring (New York: Ballentine Books, 1954, 1973) p.160.

The Scorpion, Legend of the Five Rings, by Stephen D. Sullivan has central themes of witchcraft, pagan worship, divination, spells, curses, and much more. Wizards of the Coast own the rights to this book and produce many popular fantasy games such as Dungeons and Dragons, Ninja Turtles, Magic the Gathering, and Dual Masters, all which promote the basic teaching of witchcraft.

CRYSTAL CLEAR

These teachings are abominations according to scripture. Deuteronomy 18:9-12 says, "When thou art come into the land which the Lord thy God giveth thee, thou shalt not learn to do after the abominations of those nations. There shall not found among you any one that maketh his son or his daughter to pass through the fire, or that useth divination, or an observer of times, or an enchanter, or a witch, Or a charmer, or a consulter with familiar spirits, or a wizard, or a necromancer. For all that do these things are an abomination unto the Lord: and because of these abominations the Lord thy God doth drive them out from before thee." All of these books I just mentioned are targeted to an audience of 9 to 13-year-old children, all with the same theme of witchcraft, Satanism, and Paganism.

No matter how it is packaged, it is still the same message. Unfortunately, because many people, especially children, don't recognize occult symbols, or understand witchcraft, thousands of young readers are led to accept fantasy as harmless. Many people hold the view that in a fantasy story with good vs. evil such as The Ring series, allegories portray a veiled view of Christ seeming willingly to ignore the occultic themes in the story. But in our presentation of the Gospel, should we try to veil the message of Christ or should we make it crystal clear? Our society is completely different now than it was back in 1940. Occultism, witchcraft, and Satanism are so wide spread now in today's culture we must contend for the truth of the Gospel. If we don't take a spiritual stand, who will?

Look at this in Jude 3, it says, "Beloved, when I gave all diligence to write unto you of the common salvation, it was needful for me to write unto you, and exhort you that ye should earnestly contend for the faith which was once delivered unto the saints." This scripture urges us to stand against any attack against the truth of the Gospel of Christ, whether it is a veiled view or an all out blatant attack of Satanism, Occultism, or Paganism. You might say, "Can a simple fantasy book really affect my life? I have so many friends who read books like we've been talking about and they don't seem to be affected by them?"

You might not see the effects immediately, but if you look back on the facts we've talked about, obviously the message behind some of these fantasy books have affected a lot of people, especially younger children. One of the things that are so deceptive about the power of the occult is that it is so subtle and undetectable until one day you are really involved in its power without ever really even knowing it. The Bible calls these spirits "seducing spirits." Besides the facts we've talked already about, the Bible gives us many examples about how to deal with the propagation of occultic material. Let's take a look.

"Many of them also which used curious arts brought their books together, and burned them before all men" Acts 19:19. This scripture goes on to indicate that the value of these books were fifty thousand pieces of silver, or about 138 years of wages for a rural laborer.

Why would they burn books with such monetary value? It was because these people who practiced occultism and witchcraft with these books knew themselves that there was a spiritual release that took place when the content of the book was released. In other words, there was spiritual power behind the book. Fantasy books, especially ones written by occultic authors can have the same effect on an individual as these books they burned in Acts. It is the same content, just packaged different.

JUST ONE WORD

Early in my Christian life I was experiencing tormenting thoughts that were driving me crazy. I prayed, I fasted, I read the Word and they still wouldn't go away. I went to a church service and the pastor gave an altar call that was just for me. As I went down to the altar to respond a lady was at the front, as well. She gave the pastor a "word of knowledge" about my situation. A "word of knowledge" is one of the gifts of the Holy Spirit and it's where a particular word is given to someone about your situation by the Holy Spirit to help in the problem. It's found in 1 Corinthians 14. She said I had a book in my house that was occultic and it was opening a doorway for evil spirits to torment me. I went home found a book and disposed of it. I repented for having the book, covered my house in the blood of Jesus, and rebuked these demonic spirits in Jesus name. Immediately the oppression stopped.

The Word of God, which is the Sword of the Spirit, cuts the chains from any occultic bondage that could be affecting you. That is why it is so important to read your Bible daily. When I was young, I always was told to read my Bible every day. What I didn't understand is that if I filled my head with occultic messages instead of God's Word, a stronghold could be set up in my thinking, blinding my understanding of God and Jesus Christ. When a person repents of his sins and involvement with occultic practices of any kind, renounces all involvement, and receives Jesus as his Savior through His blood, he is protected from things like the occult.

Chapter 5
BEHIND THE SCREEN OF VIDEO GAMES

THE HISTORY

For decades now video games have become a permanent part of American and other cultures. Starting out with the era of Atari, video games have exploded over the past 25 years into such a worldwide spectrum of brands and games that it is hard to keep up with them and some of the games out are phenomenal. The X-Box 360 and PSP systems are crazy when it comes to graphics. Whether you are a "Gamer", or just like to play every now and then, video games are fun, interactive, and exciting. They are great to play when you are bored or just as a hobby. Playing video games has become a favorite American pastime. But just where did video games originate? How did the industry grow into what it is now?

First let's take a look at the history of video games. In 1958, William Higinbotham created the very first video game ever called "Tennis for Two." In 1962, Steve Russell invented Space War, which was the first game intended for computer use. In 1971, Nolan Bushnell and Ted Dabney created the first arcade game called "Computer Space," based on Steve Russell's Space War. They also created "Pong" in 1972. In 1972 Nolan Bushnell and Ted Dabney started a company called "Atari Computers." On June 17, 1980, Ataris' "Asteroids" and "Lunar Lander" were the first two video games ever to be registered in the copyright office. From 1980 until 2003 the video game market growth was valued at approximately $18 billion in the US alone.[46] State universities are now offering degrees in video game development and people are packing the classes out.

There are many different types of video games. Video games will fall into one of four different categories: 1. Strategy, 2. Action, 3. Sports, and 4. Racing. A best selling game will sell 1 million copies worldwide; 4 million is considered a top hit. An expansion or sequel helps extend the title of a game's popularity. Example: Pokémon, in 1999 had five different versions on the market for a total of 24 million copies that sold that year. 8% of all games sold in 2002 were expansions or sequels. A best selling expansion or sequel must reach over 20 million worldwide.[47] 49% of all video games preferred were Fantasy Role Playing (FRPG) games according to Dr. Jean Funk. FRPG's fall into the strategy category, which is very

---

[46] Jose Antonio Vargas, "Halo 2 Ready to Run Rings around Video Game Industry" Washington Post 9 November 2004: A1.
[47] Scholastic Kid's Almanac for the 21st Century (New York: Scholastic Inc., 2000) p.178.

important to understand. In 2002, 219 million video games were sold. 46 million were strategy, 37.2 million were action, 32.8 million were sports, and 21.9 million were racing. More than 87% of people who purchased video games in 2002 were 18 years old or older, which destroys the myth that video games are just for kids![48] Strategy games have a common theme of the battle between good and evil.

Some examples of the more popular games are: Pokémon's Sapphire and Ruby, The Sims, Madden NFL, Final Fantasy X, Grand Theft Auto 3 and Vice City, XXX BMX, Mirra BMX2, Tony Hawks ProSkater, Halo, Harry Potter, Enter the Matrix, Desert Storm, Diablo II, and WarCraft.

THE RESEARCH

As exciting and entertaining as video games have become, what are the affects some video games can have on our society and is it possible for some video games to impact your spiritual life? Let's take a look at some facts. One in seven teens is addicted to video games. A 15-year study was done by psychologist Albert Bandura on social learning and the tendency of children to imitate what they see. As a result of this study, in 1969, the Surgeon General, formed the Scientific Advisory Committee on Television and Social Behavior. It was formed to assess the impact of violence on attitudes, values, and behavior of the viewers. A report given by this committee said this about children seeing violence on TV: 1. Children may become less sensitive to the pain and suffering of others, 2. Children

---

[48] Scholastic Kid's Almanac for the 21st Century p.178.

may be more fearful of the world around them; 3. Children may be more likely to behave in aggressive or harmful ways towards others.[49]

Research by Psychologist L.R. Huesman and others found that children who watched many hours of violence on television when they were in elementary school tended to also show a higher level of aggressive behavior when they became teenagers. Following these teens into adulthood, they found that ones who'd watched a lot of violence when they were 8 years old were more likely to be arrested and prosecuted for criminal acts as adults.

Wow, that's crazy! A typical child in the U.S. watches 28 hours of TV a week. Seeing as many as 8,000 murders by the time they finish elementary school at age 11 and even worse, the killers are depicted as getting away with the murders 75% of the time, while showing no remorse.[50] A USA Today article (Laura Parker and Donna Leinwand, "Tarot Card's Meaning, If Any, Undermined," USA Today, October 10, 2002) about clues left behind during the Washington, DC suburban sniper shootings back in 2002, states that where a 13-year-old boy was shot and wounded near to a middle school in Bowie, MD, there was a shell casing and a hand written message on a tarot card that said, "Dear policeman, I am God."

---

[49] C.A. Anderson, N.L. Carnagey, & J. Eubanks. "Exposure to Violent Media: The Effects of Songs with Violent Lyrics on Aggressive Thoughts and Feelings," Journal of Personality and Psychology 84:5 (2003).
[50] L.R. Hesumann, J. Moise-Titus, C.L. Podolski, & L.D. Eron. "Longitudinal Relations Between Children's Exposure to TV Violence and their Aggressive and Violent Behavior in Young Adulthood," Developmental Psychology 39:2 (2003) p.201-221.

The article goes on to say, "Tarot cards also are used in several popular fantasy role playing games. In one, "Deux: You are a God", a player assumes the identity of one of 36 gods, and a tarot card defines powers. Characters use the cards to advance their schemes to alter events in the mortal world. Criminologists say the phrase, "I am God" often is used by players of video games to indicate mastery of a particular game. An entire line of video games involves simulations that allow players to essentially play God by creating and destroying things."[51]

The article essentially indicates that authorities believed this sniper was involved in video games of this nature. I believe this. I was counseling one young man who had a friend who was playing a Pokémon video game so much that he would yell out, "I am the Dragon Master" in his school halls. One day someone yelled back "I'm the Dragon Slayer" and the young man who played Pokémon tried to stab the boy with a pen and actually kill him.

As I've stated earlier the research by psychologist Craig A. Anderson shows playing violent video games can increase a person's aggressive thoughts, feelings, and behavior both in laboratory settings and in actual life. The study Dr. Anderson did in 2000 suggests that violent video games may be more harmful than violent television and movies because they are interactive, very engrossing, and require the player to identify with the aggressor. Dr. Anderson was quoted as saying, "One major conclusion from this and other research on violent entertainment media is that content matters." Anderson says, "This message is

[51] Laura Parker & Donna Leinward, "Tarot Card's Meaning, if any, Undetermined," <u>USA Today</u> 10 October 2002.

important for all consumers, but especially for parents of children and adolescents."[52]

So, in other words, all the research shows that video games can be very dangerous in affecting one's behavior if the message is violent or a negative message? As I've mentioned before, on a recent news television talk show "Anderson and Cooper" on CNN, an interviewee that researched all of the high school killers like Columbine, CO., found that all of the killers played violent video games and listened to violent music lyrics.[53] There have been over 1000 studies done on the affects violent media have on the consumer, especially children. All 1000 of these studies proved that negative media does affect the consumer to one degree or another.

THE GAMES

I've studied the affects of violent and satanic music lyrics for years and without a doubt we have found the same result. The reason video games are even more consuming and involving is because they make the person become interactive with the game's message. All the research over the past 10 years has led to ratings for video games such as: E for Everyone, T for Teen, M for Mature, A for Adults Only, and C for Early Childhood. Each has a subtitle that describes the content for each game. ESRB stands for Entertainment Software Rating Board.

Although the rating system has helped a lot in describing the content of video games, it does not define any spiritual content at all. Any type of witchcraft or occultism slips through the system. Some of these games

---

[52] Anderson, Carnagey, & Eubanks
[53] "Teen Killers," <u>Anderson Cooper 360,</u> Fox News, 22 March 2005.

have warnings about causing epileptic seizures while playing the games. Remember earlier we said that 49% of all video games were strategy/fantasy games? Games like Final Fantasy X, WarCraft III, Resident Evil, Harry Potter and the Prisoner of Azkaban, any of the Pokémon games, and The Legend of Dargon are all examples of strategy/fantasy games, which make up 49% of the video games industry.

One important thing to know is that a lot of these games teach you the fundamentals of witchcraft while playing the games. For instance, all the Final Fantasy games teach: 1. About tarot cards and how to read and understand their powers, 2. How to summon demons with spells and incantations, 3. How to create spells using elements, stones, and crystals (The satanic pentagram represents the four elements: earth, fire, wind, water, and the fifth is spirit, which represents the spirit released by the spells.), 4. How to astral project or to travel in the spirit outside your body with the help of supernatural demonic power. Listen to this.

On the "Final Fantasy VII" it says "magic, while you are in the menu screen; you can cast magic for recovery, cure, and check magic like 'summon' or 'enemy skill'…Choose this command to use magic. After selecting the magic decide upon whom the magic will be cast. Magic spells available to you are displayed in the white while those that cannot be used are displayed in gray.[54] In order to cast each magic, Materia must be equipped on the character's weapons or armor. 'Summon,' displays the available Summon magic (Summon monsters) and their

---

[54] Final Fantasy 7, computer software handbook, Sony Entertainment, Soft Square, 1997.

effects. In order to cast the Summon Magic, Summon Materia must be attached to character's weapons or armor... materia. If material orbs are inserted into slots in weapons or armor, various abilities become available. Select this command in order to equip the Materia or to see its abilities...[55] Materia, magic material, green material. This will enable you to cast a number of Attack Magic and Curative Magic, Summon Materia, Red Materia. This will enable you to cast Summon Magic during battle, in order to call a Summon Monster.[56] Elements, by equipping certain weapons, armor and accessories, each character can gain special elemental abilities useful for both offense and defense. When the character obtains these elements the name of each element is shown on white. The nine elements are fire, ice, lighting, earth, poison, gravity, water, wind, and holy."[57]

OPENING A DOOR FOR A CURSE

If we have social and medical evidence that validate the idea that video games can affect you after periods of meditation, what do you think happens to your spirit after meditating on something that the Bible directly tells you to have nothing to do with? Deuteronomy 7: 25-26 NIV says, "The images of their gods you are to burn in the fire. And do not take it for yourselves, or you will be ensnared by it, for it is detestable to the Lord your God. Do not bring a detestable thing into your house or you, like it, will be set

---

[55] Final Fantasy 7, p.33
[56] Final Fantasy 7, p.34
[57] Final Fantasy 7, p.36

apart for destruction. Utterly abhor and detest it, for it is set apart for destruction."

What this scripture is saying is that we are supposed to hate things that promote occultism and witchcraft, but instead our culture has completely embraced these things and we are paying billions a year to do so. When you purchase a video game with occultic propaganda, such as symbols and basic concepts, you are opening a door for a curse to come on your entire house. Not only that but the more you play the games, the more you become desensitized to occultic practices.

Think about it, instead of meditating on God's Word, as we are suppose to do, we have a whole generation meditating on games like these for hours a day. The average person consumes 7 hours of media a day. These games teach occultism and games like XXX BMX and Grand Theft Auto promote violence, sexual perversion, and sorcery. If the media that you consume is like this, it can eventually have an effect on your Spirit man.

I have personally met and counseled with teenagers who have become heavily demonically oppressed to the point of having almost no control over their actions as a direct result of playing certain occultic video games. Some have actually been placed in group homes directly because of the influence of the video game. (One young man experienced demonic seizures because of playing the games, but through prayer was restored!) This incident is not an isolated incident. It is actually very common in behavior modification schools. I've counseled with a young man mentally addicted to the Final Fantasy video game so much to the point he became physically aggressive and attacked his mother and father with a knife when they were trying to take the game away from him. Another young man would ditch school and forget to bathe for weeks because he would become so consumed by the Final Fantasy video games.

So, what I am saying is that playing certain occultic video games can open doors for evil spirits to work in your life! We have seen scriptural evidence as well as physical effects they can have. But are all video games bad? Of course not, that would be ridiculous to say. However the video games that are promoting evil things like witchcraft, sexual perversion, and sorcery are definitely bad!

You might ask, "What do I look for when looking for a game to play?" Look at titles. If it is talking about "Diablo" there's a good chance you shouldn't buy it. If you see concepts of magic in it, that is probably another good indicator not to purchase it. If you see occultic symbols like the pentagram, hexagram, the inverted or upright pyramid, the illuminated eye, the satanic cross, or the Goat Head, any of these signs are occultic in nature and indicate a connection to the occult. Beware! You also need to read the ratings; they usually give a fairly clear description of the content.

So what can you do to protect yourself from being affected by things like this? A lot of kids have come to me and said, "What do I do if I've already got a video game like this, I mean I don't want to open a spiritual door for the demonic? What do I do?"

The first step is to repent of your sins and all involvement in activities like this and to apply the Blood of Jesus over them. Renounce those activities with the intent of not doing them ever again, and receive Jesus as your Lord and Savior if you're not a Christian. The evidence is clearly laid out that what your mind ingests can affect you emotionally and spiritually.

Chapter 6
BEHIND BODY ART: TATTOOS

TATTOOS TODAY

Tattoos can be a very touchy subject in today's culture because there is a very strong argument on both sides of the debate over the morality of tattoos. In the past ten years tattoos have exploded in our culture as one of the leading retail businesses. According to US News and World Report, tattooing is the country's sixth fastest growing retail business, and it is growing by the rate of more than one new tattoo studio everyday.[58] Over 39 million Americans have a tattoo. From television to toys, tattoos are everywhere and it seems to have been labeled as "the thing to do." Think about how many celebrities you know that have a tattoo. Just about every Rock star has one. Some stars include Britney Spears, Pamela Anderson, Tiger Woods, and the all-American hero, Michael Jordan. As a matter of fact, an

---

[58] "Tattoos," <u>US News and World Report</u> 3 November 1997.

AP poll taken discovered that 35% of all NBA players have at least one tattoo. What is the average age when getting a tattoo? Believe it or not, 16 years old. The average reason people get one is to express something, or to cover up a scar.

No matter how you slice it or dice it, the tattoo that once was a sign of criminal and social outcasts, has quickly become one of the most commonly accepted forms of art in American society. Remember the rap star from back in the late 80's named "Vanilla Ice." When he first came out, it was clean uniforms and fancy moves. Now the moves are still there and the tattoos are from head to toe. This is an example of the change that has taken place in our culture. As tattoos arise in our culture so do a lot of questions about the art. What exactly is a tattoo? Where did they come from? Are they safe? Is it okay for a Christian to get a tattoo or are all tattoos a form of evil?

MARKED FOR JESUS?

An enormous amount of Judeo-Christian tattoo studios are popping up all over the nation a long with some of these hard hitting unanswered questions by our nation's youth. Just recently I was talking to a friend in Atlanta, GA. When I first met this guy he was addicted to cocaine and never, never ever went to church, much less ever accepted Jesus as Savior. He started coming to some Bible studies that I was holding. The young man was delivered from addiction and started to radically follow Jesus Christ. After a few years, he was still doing great and on fire with the Holy Spirit. He debated about going on the mission field out of the country. He was genuine about his desire to spread the Gospel, so much that he would go on the streets of downtown Atlanta and talk to people about Jesus. He would even hold up signs that said, "Will work for Jesus" during rush hour and after Atlanta Braves games, reaching thousands of people with God's love. He is a musician and he came to me one day and asked me if I thought it would be okay to get a scripture tattooed on his body to further evangelize and express his devotion to Jesus Christ. I have many friends and know people in my church who have Christian symbols tattooed on their body as well. I know many very anointed Christian musicians with religious tattoos and I know this is a very popular trend in Christian music, as well as this up and coming generation of Christians. These questions are as genuine and sincere as these people's faith in God.

Many people are getting "marked for Jesus" as this American phenomenon grows. I've been asked by many youth and adults these questions that I just shared with you. Before I answer that, let's talk about this, "What is a tattoo and where did they come from? The Latin word for tattoo is "stigma" and the original meaning is reflected in modern dictionaries. Among the definitions of "stigma" listed by Webster are "a prick with a pointed instrument, a distinguishing mark cut into the flesh of a slave or a criminal, and a mark of disgrace or reproach."[59]

THE HISTORY

Historically, tattoos have been around as long as man has. From Siberia, Japan, and Egypt, tattoos have been found in tombs on mummies dating back thousands of years. More recently, in 1717, branding was abolished in

---

[59] Steve Gilbert, Tattoo History: A Source Book (Powerhouse Books, 2001) p.15

the army and replaced with tattooing...with the letter "D" for deserter. In the Greek and Roman culture, tattoos were used to mark slaves and criminals, so they could be identified if they tried to escape. It was ancient Japanese tradition to tattoo convicted criminals, as well. By the 1900's, tattooing had reached the United States as a sideshow attraction in circuses.

By the mid 1900's, sailors were using tattoos to show what part of the world they had sailed.[60] As the late 1900's came around, tattoos tended to become generally more accepted in American culture. Now tattoos are worn by business people, politicians, musicians, movie stars, and athletes. From magazines to MTV, tattoos are a very common and accepted thing in our society.

One very popular tattoo, which is big in the underground scene and I mean very underground, is known as the "jail house" tattoo. Children do not try this at home! I've had friends incarcerated in America's prison systems that have received tattoos underground style. The ink? Burnt styrofoam captured on notebook paper mixed with toothpaste! The tattoo gun? A motor made out of a broken tape player. The needle? An unfolded paper clip attached to the end of the motor, powered by the batteries of the tape deck. Just a mental note, I've seen most all of these tattoos messed up very badly and all with amazing stories of what happened. Like I said before, don't try this at home!

THE RESEARCH

A question I had to ask myself is, "No matter how widespread tattoos are, are they safe? And what are some

---

[60] Gilbert, p.15.

facts about tattoos?" Check this out! Young people with tattoos are four more times likely to engage in sexual intercourse, over two times more likely to experience alcohol related problems, two times more likely to use illegal drugs, over two times more likely to express violent behavior and over two times more likely to drop out of high school.[61] The doctor, Dr. Timothy A. Roberts, who conducted this study, has a tattoo himself and his whole purpose behind the study was to disprove unfair stereotypes of people with tattoos. He was quoted as saying "I was more than a little surprised at the result." After the study he said, "A tattoo is a sign that doctors, parents, and teachers ought to be asking about teenagers' behavior." Another study done in Denmark found that 42% of people in homes for short-term detention were tattooed, as were 60% in homes for young men with behavior difficulties, 72% in prisons for young men and 52% of all Denmark prison populations. Studies also show that people with personality disorders frequently have multiple small tattoos.[62]

What about the health dangers of having a tattoo? Hepatitis C kills over 10,000 people per year in the U.S. Currently, 4 million Americans have hepatitis C. "According to a report out by the Center for Disease Control (CDC), "the innocent" commercial tattoo may be the number one distributor of hepatitis C. The American Red Cross prohibits blood donors from donating blood for

---

[61] Timothy A. Roberts, M.D. & Sheryl A. Ryan, M.D., "Tattooing and High Risk Behavior In Adolescents," published study, Division of Adolescence Medicine, Strong Children's Research Center, University of Rochester School of Medicine, Rochester, NY.
[62] Ronald Scutt, <u>Art, Sex, and Symbol</u> 1974, p.115

12 months- one complete year- after getting tattooed."[63]
"According to research published in the Journal of School
Health, 70% of 642 adolescents surveyed in a study
reported hemorrhaging while being tattooed."[64] The CDC
recently received a question asking if someone could get
HIV from a tattoo. The reply was, "A risk of HIV
transmission does exist if instruments contaminated with
blood are either not sterilized or disinfected or are used
inappropriately between clients and few states have
hygienic regulations to ensure safe tattooing practices in
commercial tattoo parlors, and even fewer monitor and
enforce standards."[65]

There are some tattoo parlors that do have clean
hygienic practices and there are some people in the industry
that work hard to make their practices safe as possible. I
personally have experienced professional tattoo artists that
have tried to change the reputation of the industry.
However, because of the lack of standards, accountability,
and evaluation of the industry, the industry as a whole, has
a lot of work to do to get the practice of tattooing regulated
as a "safe" practice.

There is a lot of legislation in process across the nation
to change the practices of the industry as a whole. In many
states, tattooing is, or has been made, legal. South Carolina
for instance, which has recently legalized tattooing, is just
now setting, developing and setting up standards. But until

---

[63] R.W. Harley & R.P. Fischer, "Commercial Tattooing as Potential Source of
Hepatitis C Infection," Medicine Issue 80(March 2000): p.134-151.
[64] Donald Staffo, The Tuscaloosa Times 10 January 2001.
[65] Laura Raybold, Everything You Need To Know About the Dangers of
Tattooing and Body Piercing, p.18

the boundaries of the industry have been set and enforced, the reputation of the industry will not change.

TO TATTOO OR NOT TO TATTOO

You might say, "Well, maybe there are some health risks involved but what about the question, "Are tattoos evil? Or, are they just a way of expressing oneself?" There are many people in the Christian community that would and could argue both sides of this debate extremely well. Christians that are pro-tattoo will argue that it is a form of expressing their devotion to Christ. Often they quote scriptures like Revelation 19:16 that say, "On his robe and on his thigh he has a name (Jesus) inscribed, King of Kings and Lord of Lords."

Also, Revelation 7:2-4 which talks about the servants of God having a seal in their foreheads after the Rapture says, "And I saw another angel ascending from the east, having the seal of the Living God: and he cried with a loud voice to the four angels to whom it was given to hurt the earth and the sea, Saying, hurt not the earth, neither the sea, nor the trees, till we have sealed the servants of our God in their foreheads. And I heard the number of them which were sealed: and there were sealed a hundred and forty and four thousand of all the tribes of the children of Israel."

This is called "tattoo imagery" in the Bible. Also, pro-tattoo Christians will argue the difference between the Old Law and the New Law. Others say that tattoos are an expression of evangelism, which every believer is commanded to do. For example, before the New Testament believers could not eat pork and certain meats, but after the New Testament, the Holy Spirit revealed to Peter by an open vision of a different era. This vision was given to symbolize an era of God reaching out to other people besides the Jews. So, many people who use this concept to support tattooing say that now under the New Testament teachings, "grace" takes away the Law that commanded no markings on the body in the Old Testament.

On the other hand, anti-tattoo Christian thoughts include, "Ye shall not make any cuttings in your flesh for the dead, nor print any marks other upon you. I am the Lord" Leviticus 19:28 and many other scriptures along this line, as well. One, for example, is I Corinthians 6:19-20 that says, "Know ye not that your body is the temple of the Holy Ghost which is in you, which ye have of God, and ye are not your own? For ye are bought with a price: therefore glorify God in your body, and in your spirit, which are God's." There is also very powerful historical evidence that tattoos originated in connection with the satanic practice of blood letting. From Pro-Non-Christian Tattoo sources, "Tattooing had originated in connection with ancient rites of scarification and blood letting which were associated with religious practices intended to put the human soul in harmony with supernatural forces."[66] "Blood that is let is believed to unleash power." People practicing bloodletting believe there is a spiritual release as the blood is released that invokes demonic forces. Many people who practice witchcraft do practice blood letting through the process of tattooing! There is a lot of scriptural, historical, medical, and social evidence that tattoos are used for evil purposes.[67]

---

[66] Steve Gilbert, p.158
[67] Rosemary Ellen Guiley, The Encyclopedia of Witches and Witchcraft, Second Edition, (Facts On File, Inc., 1999) p.26

Again, you might say, "But what if the tattoo is a Christian tattoo? Is it okay for a Christian to get one then? I mean I have a lot of friends who have tattoos and say that there is nothing wrong with it." My answer would be to take a look at the social and medical facts. I received a tattoo shortly after making a vow to Satan to signify my vow, which is alarmingly not uncommon. A lot of Rock and Rap artists have done this and apparently the list includes "Eminem" and "The Game" from G-Unit.

THE BOTTOM LINE

The bottom line question to ask yourself is "Why do you really want a tattoo?" Are you already evangelizing and glorifying Jesus in your life in other ways to the best of your ability? Would you offend other believers that might not believe it is biblically okay to get a tattoo? Or is it because you want one for selfish or rebellious reasons?

No matter if you have occultic tattoos or not, Jesus loves you and washes away all your sin with the blood that He shed on the cross for your sins. Revelation 1:5-6 says, "And from Jesus Christ, who is the faithful witness, and the first begotten of the dead, and the prince of the kings of the earth. Unto him that loved us, and washed us from our sins in his own blood, And hath made us kings and priests unto God and his Father; to him be glory and dominion for ever and ever. Amen." No matter what your choice would be about the biblical validity of having a tattoo, make sure your heart and motives are right in the process, consider the health risk and understand that tattoos don't wash off!

Shawn Patrick Williams

Chapter 7
THE CULTURE OF HIP-HOP: RAP MUSIC

THE LO-DOWN

What is Rap and Hip-Hop music? Who listens to it? What's really behind some of the messages coming from the culture? 65% of everyone between the ages of 13 and 24 listen to Rap and Hip-Hop music. With record sales of 635.8 million units (CDs or cassettes) sold in 2003, Rap music has definitely made its mark in American culture. That's over 8 billion dollars in sales, which ten years ago would have made up the entire music market. These figures do not include the rapidly growing trend of music downloading over the Internet. In 2003, 21.7 million albums were legally downloaded off the Internet with a growth rate of 20% up from 2002. Rap music DVD sales have soared with a 104% increase in sales for 2003. You can find Rap popping its head up virtually everywhere in our culture. The most popular Rap album in 2003, 50 Cent's "Get Rich, Or Die Tryin" sold 6.5 million, which was followed up recently by the movie with the same title. 2003, also brought Outkast's "Speakerboxxx/The Love Below" 3 million in sales and Beyonce's "Dangerously in Love" selling 2.5 million copies. Rap music has had a loud voice in a rough market.[68]

But just what is Rap music and where did it come from? Rap music is a form of rhyming lyrics spoken rhythmically over musical instruments, with a musical backdrop of sampling, scratching, and mixing by DJs. Originally rapping was called "MCing." Rap music is one of the elements in the Hip-Hop culture. Hip-Hop is a cultural movement that began amongst urban African American youths in New York City and has since spread around the world. The four main elements in Hip-Hop are MCing, DJing, graffiti art, and break dancing. The term Hip-Hop has since come to be a synonym for Rap music to mainstream audiences, although "rapping", or Mcing, is just a vocal expression of the Hip-Hop culture.

THE ORIGINS OF HIP-HOP

Rap music started in 1970 with Jamaican born DJ Kool Herc. He moved to New York in the 60's and would chant things in between records. This type of crowd pleaser was known as "rapping" to the crowd. The first Rap record was 1979's "King Tim III" by Fatback band. The SugarHill Gang followed the same year with "Rapper's Delight" which became a major hit and is based on Chic's off-

---

[68] Barry Wills, "US Music Industry Holding Steady," Stereophile 5 January 2004.

sampled disco track "Good Times." "Rappers Delight" went on to become the best selling 12-inch record ever, selling over 2 million copies worldwide. In 1982, Grand Master Flash, the founding father of scratching, offered a demo to a group called "The Furious Fire." Their album, "The Message," went on to sell over a million copies and it was the first Rap record to describe the hopelessness felt in America's ghettos. Later that next year in 1983, Grand Master Flash and Melle Mel recorded the hard hitting anti-cocaine single "White Lines, Don't Do It", which received huge international attention because of it's description of America's projects. In a few short years, Hip-Hop came from the underground and hit the mainstream hard. A huge hit single called "Planet Rock, by Afrika Bambaata Assim, joined electronic sounds mixed with Rap. "Planet Rock" sold 620,000 copies in the US alone.

THE EVOLUTION

Not only was dance music shifted into another gear, but also a whole new dance culture was born. Along came Hip-Hop crews, graffiti artists, and break dancing. In 1983, Hip-Hop began to spread into other forms of music. In the 80's groups like "2 Live Crew" emerged with much controversial discussion about the graphic nature of the lyrics. Their album "As Nasty as They Wanna Be" was the first Rap album in the U.S. to be deemed as "obscene" in law courts. 2 Live Crew appealed on the grounds of free speech. Run DMC exploded on the Rap scene with their new style of Rap, gold chains, and sportswear. They had a hit song called "My Adidas," in which the shoe company Adidas paid Run DMC a six figure sum to wear their clothes, making them the first band to be sponsored by a clothing company. As the years went on, so did the evolution of the Hip-Hop movement. Guys like KRS-1, LL Cool J, The Beastie Boys, Public Enemy, and NWA all emerged in the 80's, each with their own style of rapping. NWA stood for "Niggas with an Attitude" and based all their lyrics on violence, drugs, and guns receiving instant negative media coverage. Public Enemy based their style on the Afro-American organization, The Black Panthers. "Fight The Power" was one of Public Enemy's many rap anthems that lead to an FBI report examining Rap effects on national security.

A "hard core" trend had been set in the 80's and drug, sex, and guns seemed to be the leading Rap solution for cultural problems. Throughout the 90's, the trend just increased. Dr. Dre, Ice Cube, Ice-T, Tupac Shakur, Easy-E, Cypress Hill, Snoop Dogg, The Wu-Tang Clan, Bone Thugs-N-Harmony, NAS, Notorious BIG, and many more artists made their mark in the 90's and now in the millennium, Eminen, 50 Cents, Lil John, Ludicrous, DMX, Jay-Z, and Outkast have become American household names.[69] But what's really behind this cultural Hip-Hop machine?

The rapper "Chuck D" from the rap group Public Enemy, who had the huge hit song "Fight the Power," was quoted as saying, "There's a real thin line between fantasy and reality... When you are not in control of your reality, fantasy becomes a bigger influence... The low road is easier to walk as a recording artist. A lot of rappers wouldn't get the time of day from record producers if they

---

[69] Alan Light, "Vibe History of Hip-Hop," <u>Vibe Magazine</u> 1999.

weren't doing negative rap…"[70] One of Chuck's songs led to an FBI report examining raps effect on national security. The actor/rapper named Ludicrous sings a song called "Cold Outside." The song starts out, "To my niggas on the block on the grind and hustlin trying to sell some (crack) rocks." He goes on to rap, "I'm hiding out smoking herb (marijuana) because my boss is getting on my mother******* nerves… they be cutting them bodies on slab. They be putting those bodies in bags…want to disrespect give me your neck and I'll out a knife in it."[71] The song is talking about the glorification of drugs and cold-blooded murder.

ONE THIRTY-MINUTE CONCERT

On February 2004, in Kissimmee, FL. at a local high school, two students were killed in a drag racing accident and a teacher died of breast cancer. The school board and the principle decided to let Ludicrous perform a 30-minute concert to the student body of 2,000 children to "lift up their spirits."[72] Ludicrous has a LP called "Chicken and Beer" and in a song on it, he says, "I try to stay focused and clean, but I got a little dope and some green," referring to marijuana.[73]

---

[70] Nathan McCall, What's Going On? (New York: Random House, 1997).
[71] Ludicras, Word of Mouth, compact disc, The Island of DefJam Music Group, 2001, Song 14.
[72] Music Television Videos, MTV News
[73] Ludicras, Chicken-n-Beer, compact disc, The Island of DefJam Music Group, 2003, Song 7.

THE ARTISTS

One of the most popular Rappers out there today is 50 Cent. On one of his albums, 50 Cent has a song called "High All the Time," which was produced by a guy named Triple Beam, which is what drug dealers use to weigh out drugs, particularly cocaine. A song off his album, which stayed at the top of the charts for months, was called "In Da Club." The lyrics read, "I've got the X (ecstasy) if you into taking drugs." On another song, he sings, "My songs belong in the Bible with King David."[74] The Rappers Dr. Dre and Eminem together produced this album of 50 Cent. 50 cent started a group called "G-Unit", which I'll talk about later. On 50 Cent's album, "The Massacre" released in 2005, the cover carries a picture of 50 Cent counting money with a triple beam with cocaine on it on a table. There are also pictures of 50 Cent and members of G-Unit shooting guns at people out of the car window. Lyrics on a track called "Funz Come Out" say, "when I come through your projects 187's (a drive by shooting) in progress. Hard niggas tend to soften up when that lead touch-em." The song "A Baltimore Love Thing" is all about a girl hooked on crack and inside the album it has a crack pipe in her hand. 50 Cent says, "When we first met I thought you'd never doubt me, now you're trying to leave me, you'll never live without me."[75]

Earl Simmons, better known as DMX, has made a big career of rapping and acting as well. Starting out with "Murder, Inc." in the late 90's, he made raps that eventually launched a very lucrative solo career. The message DMX

---

[74] 50 Cent, <u>Get Rich, Or Die Tryin'</u>, compact disc,
Shady/Aftermath/Interscope Records, Song 5.
[75] 50 Cent, <u>The Massacre</u>, compact disc, Shady/G-Unit/Interscope Records, 2005.

raps about is a very mixed message. On his 1999 album "And Then There Was X" he has prayer to Jesus Christ about using his talents to lead people to Jesus, but on the very same album he sings about the glorification of violence and sex. In a Source magazine interview, he talks about selling his soul to Satan and off his own LP says, "It's dark and hell is hot."[76] He sings about the event on a track called "Damion." He also has a song about practicing necrophilia, which says, "I've got blood on ***** cause I **** a corpse. I got blood on my ***** and there's no remorse." He also sings songs about rape. "I'm coming to your house and I'm gunning for your spouse, if you got a daughter older than 15 I'm gonna rape her right there on the living room floor."[77]

Another rapper from Atlanta, GA by the name of "Bone Crusher" put out an LP called "Attenchun" in 2003 from SoSo Def Records and Breakem Off Records. The entire content of the album contains glorification of murder, drug dealing, sex, and hypocritical religious references. On the song entitled, "Vain Glorious" the artist sings "A lot of people told me I couldn't make this **** happen... If you believe in your **** you can make your **** happen because everything's possible through God." On a very popular song called "Never Scared," TI made a guest appearance and sang about shooting someone and putting them in ICU after they were dying and shaking on the pavement. He sings, "I tell you what if you make it call it

---

[76] DMX, <u>And Then There Was X</u>, compact disc, The DefJam Music Group, 1999.

[77] <u>They Sold Their Souls for Rock-N-Roll</u>, videocassette, Fight the Good Fight Ministries, 2001 (240 min.)

grace cause it's amazing... I do this **** like a priest, confess and never seize."[78]

THEIR MESSAGE

The message coming out from much of the Rap culture is the same. It includes murder, drugs, sex, and/or a very hypocritical view of God and Jesus Christ. But is all of the culture saying the same thing? Can these negative rap lyrics have a negative affect on your behavior if you listen to them? What are the facts about the culture and what are the myths?

In a study done on March 3, 2003, Emory University's Rollins School of Public Health concluded that teens that spend more time watching the sex and violence depicted in the "real" life of "gangsta" Rap music videos are more likely to practice those behaviors in real life. After studying 522 black girls between the ages of 14 and 18 from non-urban, lower socioeconomic neighborhoods, researchers found that the girls who viewed these gangsta videos for at least 14 hours per week were far more likely to practice a number of destructive behaviors. They were 3 times more likely to hit a teacher, over 2.5 times more likely to get arrested, twice as likely to have multiple sexual partners, 1.5 times more likely to get an STD, use drugs or drink alcohol.[79] Another study found children between ages 2 and 18 spend seven hours a day ingesting some sort of media. Susan Buttrous, MD, chief of child development and behavioral pediatrics at the University of Mississippi

---

[78] Bone Crusher, <u>Attenchun</u>, So-So Def Records, 2003.
[79] Ralph J. DiClemente Ph.D., professor of Public Health, Emory University, Atlanta, GA., <u>American Journal of Public Health</u> March 2003,

Medical Center said, "We know that with any type of repeated media exposure, desensitization can occur that makes these behaviors seem normal." Buttrous also wrote a policy statement that found 75% of rap music videos contained sexual imagery and more than half involved violence, usually against women. There have been nearly 1,000 studies that have looked at the effects that media have on children's behaviors and nearly all of them find that there is a strong effect.[80]

The University of California at Berkeley, School of Public Health, conducted research on how alcohol has been portrayed in Rap music and videos. The project took 343 of the most popular Rap songs recorded between 1979 and 1997. They also looked at 112 radio and 26 television ads for alcoholic beverages that featured Rap music and 166 of the most popular Rap videos. The results found that Rap songs containing references to alcoholic beverages increased significantly over the study period from 8% of hit songs at the beginning to 45% by 1997. It also found Rap songs portraying alcohol in a positive light over the course of the study period. In 1979, 45% of the Rap songs made drinking alcohol look good and by 1997, 74% of the songs portrayed alcohol in a positive light. The mentions of alcohol brand names increased abruptly in the mid to late 1990's with 68% of alcohol related songs, including mention of a brand name by the end of the of the study period. Basically the study showed 74% of Rap songs glorified using alcohol and 68% mentioned brand names of

---

[80] Susan Buttross, <u>American Journal of Public Health</u>, 3 March 2003.

alcohol companies.[81] That's sending a pretty strong message to a generation. The reason drugs or violence wasn't included in this grant was because the researchers couldn't accurately decode all the references to violence or drugs.

On June 21, 2004, the Committee of Censorship in the Democratic Republic of Congo censored all Congolese Rap groups and foreign music. This decision was made by the Governor of the Republic. The reason given for banning Rap is that it is "obscene and violent, and caused the youth to behave badly."[82] Basically the Government saw such a negative effect on their country's youth from Rap music and culture that they made having it illegal. That is rather serious.

In the U.S., law enforcement has noticed such a problem between crime and the Hip-Hop culture that it has started what is known as "Police Rap Intelligence." Derrick Parker, founder of the NYC Police Department Rap Intelligence Unit said, "I saw a pattern... The pattern was that the Rap music industry was becoming more like organized crime. It was running side by side with traditional steps of organized crime."[83] What he is saying is the people developing and leading this movement are behaving like an organized criminal movement. That is a strong statement!

This isn't the only time the U.S. government has taken some proactive roles in battling the Rap culture. The

---

[81] University of California at Berkley, School of Public Health, "Research On the Use of Rap Music in Alcohol Advertising and the Portrayal of Drug Abuse and Violence," published study, Issued January 2003.

[82] Nolan Strong, "Congolese Government Bans Rap and Foreign Music," All Hip-Hop News, 28 June 2004.

[83] Dasun Allah, "The Hip-Hop Cop," Village Voice, 6 April 2004.

Missouri state court was prosecuting two cases, one in 1998, which was a school rampage shooting, and one in 2002 where 2 jailers were killed in a murder trial. In both cases, the lyrics of Bone Thugs-N-Harmony's songs were submitted as the state's evidence as the inspiration of the acts of the people who listened to the lyrics, which were all about murder. After hours of getting "pumped up" on the music, they went out and actually committed murder.[84]

The studies and facts show how negative Rap lyrics can affect your behavior in a very destructive and negative way. But what about spiritually? Are there artists that are Satanic and what is their message? What does the Bible say about Rap music?

Rap artist "Marshall Mathers", aka "Eminem", released a song called "Guilty Conscience" in a 1999 album, "The Marshall Mathers Project." On the song, he sings of a voice in his conscience named "Slim Shady." He sings about fighting Slim's influence of thoughts about robbery, rape, murder, and kidnapping. In the end of the song, Slim wins the battle over Eminem's thoughts. In a Spin magazine article called, "The Devil and Mr. Mathers," Eminem refers to "the spirit of Slim Shady," as the spirit that revealed itself to him in a bathroom and the references in his song to Slim are talking about this evil spirit.[85] This practice is called "automatic writing" and is basically a demon using a person to sing through them. On his 2004 "Encore" album, he sings a song called "Evil Deeds" and it says, "Father, please forgive me, for I know not what I do, I just never had

---

[84] Music Television Videos, <u>MTV News</u>

[85] <u>They Sold Their Souls for Rock-N-Roll</u>, videocassette, Fight the Good Fight Ministries, 2001 (240 min.)

a chance to meet you. Therefore I did not know that I would grow to be my mother's evil seed and do these evil deeds... Evil deeds, while I plant these evil seeds, please release me from these demons... The camera's on, my soul is gone."[86]

Eminem has a tattoo of a demonic looking mushroom on his shoulder of Slim Shady and the record label is called Shady Records. I think it is safe to say he is purposely spreading an evil message.

Another group that is deliberately spreading a satanic influenced message is group by the name of "Three 6 Mofia." Their name came from a reference to the mark of the beast (the anti-Christ) found in Revelation 13:18. All of their lyrics are about murder, drugs, rape, and you guessed it, Satanism. In 2000, they released an album called "When the Smoke Clears Sixty Six Sixty One." On the beginning of the CD they quote scriptures about losing your soul for profit such as Proverbs 14:12, Mark 8:36, and 2 Corinthians 5:10. Immediately after quoting the scripture they say, "and those that cross thy creator will be destroyed by thy Creator 36 Mofia: sixty six sixty one."[87] They make the statement that they did sell their souls to Satan. One of their founders, "Lord Imfamous", is quoted as saying, "Ask me if I'm Satan, I'm gonna send your *** to Hell." On Three 6's 2003 LP "Da Unbreakables" he says, "Don't you know that lord can make your life a living hell and I mean the place where demon spirits dwell." This is off the track, "Testing My Gangster."

---

[86] Eminem, <u>Encore</u>, compact disc, Shady Records, 2004, Song 3.
[87] Three 6 Moffia, <u>When The Smoke Clears: Sixty6, Sixty1</u>, Loud Records/Hypnotize Minds, 2000.

If all this isn't enough to convince you that Three 6 has an evil agenda behind their music, guess who owns all the rights to their music? "Hypnotized Minds, LLC."[88] Lord Imfamous is now a part of G-Unit!

You might be asking, "Well, Shawn, it seems the whole Rap culture is bad. Are there any positive groups at all?" Yes, of course there are! Groups like: Grits, John Reuben, The Cross Movement, KJ52, The Priesthood, and these are just a few named. You can visit websites like: www.rochousecafe.org and www.tvulive.com to find out more about clean, positive Rap music.

THE GOSPEL TRUTH

What does the Bible say about Rap music? The Bible doesn't specifically say anything about Rap music, but it does say to take heed to what music you do listen to. In Mark 4 (KJV), Jesus gives us one of His most famous parables about seeds being into the heart of man. Over twelve times in this verse 25 discourse, the word "hearing" is mentioned. To sum up the parable, Jesus says in verse 24, "And He (Jesus) said unto them, 'Take heed what ye hear: with that measure ye mete, it shall be measured unto you.'" In Mark 4:24, Jesus was saying whatever seed is sown into your heart, it will grow whether good seed or bad seed. Take heed of bad seed. In verse 15 of this parable, the word "heart" in Greek is interpreted "the thoughts in a man's mind." In other words, if you are listening to six or seven hours of bad music about drugs, sex, or murder, it will eventually produce the fruit from the seed planted in your mind. These evil lyrics create what the Bible calls

---

[88] Three 6 Moffia, Hypnotize Minds LLC., 2000.

"strongholds" in your mind and can really affect you in a very negative and apparent way.

I've had kids come to me and say, "I actually can see how some of the music I listen to is affecting me negatively, but what can I do to get free from these evil thoughts?"

The answer is really simple. You must first repent for opening a door to these thoughts and you must also renew your mind by reading the Bible. Pray with me. Dear God, I come to you through the blood of Jesus and repent for all my sin, especially listening to ungodly music. I renounce all involvement from these sins, ask Jesus to be my Lord and Savior, receive the Holy Spirit into my life, and break every satanic stronghold in my mind. In Jesus name, amen.

Chapter 8
BEHIND THE WORLD OF FANTASY ROLE PLAYING GAMES: FRPGS

THE FACTS

What are FRPGs? Where did they come from? And what kind of impact are they making on the American culture? What are the facts and myths behind FRPGs? Let's look behind the world of FRPGs.

In the UK, Canada, and Australia, FRPGs are even more popular than they have been in America, which has a multi-billion dollar a year pull. A fantasy role playing game is a type of video game where players assume the roles of fictional characters via role-playing.[89] Most of FRPGs tend to focus on the behavior of the role player has assumed. At the very heart of the concept it is an interactive story telling game in which the participants engage actively

---

[89] <u>The American Heritage Dictionary of the English Language</u> (Houghton Mifflin Company) 4th Edition, 2000,2004.

making them the author, actor, and audience. In most cases fantasy role-playing games, participants play the part of characters in an imaginary world that is created and overseen by a "game master," which is like a storyteller. The storyteller or game master provides a world and characters for the players to interact with and may also be responsible for advancing a storyline, or plot that makes the game subject to very unpredictable behaviors of the players. The nature of fantasy role-playing requires the participants to be cooperative throughout the game. The players usually are not playing against each other although some do. At the end of a game session, the events that happened could be written in a book that would tell a story. There are usually rules or "game mechanics" that give characters powers and abilities in the game. While FRPGs have been around for a long time, their popularity exploded in the 70's with the phenomenon of "Dungeons and Dragons," which was a board game.

Over the decades, FRPGs have taken on many popular forms such as card and Internet video fantasy role playing games. Some popular games include: Magic the Gathering, Pokémon, Yu-Gi-Oh, and Duel Masters. Ever Quest and City of Heroes have been big hits on the massively multiplayer online games. Video games like Final Fantasy have stuck strong for a decade.

"46% of fantasy role-playing board games are aimed at 10-14 year olds. 26% are aimed at 15-17 year olds. 3/4ths of FRPGs are sold to 18-year-olds and under."[90] Typically, card FRPGs are sold to younger children because they are

---

[90] Wendell Amstutz and Steve Lansing, Ph.D., <u>Exposing and Confronting Satan and Associates</u>, 6th Edition, 1996: p.210.

easier to grasp. Your typical FRPG player is between 13 and 20. Large majorities are male, shy, sensitive, and have low social skills. Magic the Gathering, which hit the scene in 1993, has had a very similar success that Dungeon and Dragon had in the 70's. Magic the Gathering has around ½ billion cards in circulation around the world. The initial magic card set only cost $8.00. Other fantasy card role-playing games that have become very popular in the past few years are Yu-Gi-Oh, The Spell Ruler, Dark Revelation, Flaming Eternity, Duel Masters, and Shaman King- The Reincarnation. You can find the cards and FRPG's promoted from schools to fast food chains. No doubt about it, we have entered a fantasy game frenzy that is reaching our society on all levels. Magic the Gathering is even said to be a favorite past time for Microsoft employees.

There are a lot of people who claim FRPGs are harmful for children and adults to play. Is there any truth to that? What are the facts about FRPGs? Let's start with their history.

THE HISTORY

In 1913, H.G. Wells created a game called "Little Wars," which was a FRPG board game with figures that are commonly known as "miniatures." In the 1950's, Charles Roberts founded the "Avalon-Hillgames Company," which produced many FRPGs with a war theme. Because of WWII, these types of role-playing games where very successful. In the 1960's, many fantasy books like "The Lord of the Rings" were produced, which made a very big impact on the FRPG industry. In 1968, a medieval FRPG called "Chainmail" was written by Jeff Perrin and Gary Gygax. In 1971, Dave Arneson had written a set of

Napoleonic ship combat rules called, "Don't Give up the Ship." This game was published by the same company as "Chainmail". This brought about a relationship between Gary Gygax and Dave Arneson that developed into one of the most popular FRPGs that set a trend for the industry. The game? "Dungeons and Dragons." In 1973, "D&D" was published and quickly took the nation by storm. The gamers would get hooked on D&D quickly, resorting to in some cases copying the rules by Xerox because the demand had stripped the initial supply. By 1975, whole onslaughts of fantasy games were on the market, but none like D&D. The 80's brought about advanced D&D 1st and 2nd Edition. By the 90's, fantasy trading cards became very popular overshadowing the older games like D&D. One particular fantasy card game that has had the same success as D&D is "Magic the Gathering" by "Wizards of the Coast." Eventually, Wizards of the Coast bought out D&D. Wizards of the Coast went on to dominate the fantasy card industry producing games such as "Pokémon" and "Duel Masters." Many other card fantasy games are out and some like Yu-Gi-Oh are becoming very popular.

But how much do we really know about fantasy role-playing games? Can they really affect you like many have claimed? What are some facts about some of these games?

THE USER'S GUIDE INTO MAGIC 101

Here's a definition of how to use magic in the game D&D. This is taken directly from the guide written by the author of D&D, Gary Gygax. "Magic users draw upon arcane powers in order to exercise their profession...He or she must memorize and prepare for the use of each spell, and it's castings make it necessary to reabsorb the incantation by consulting the proper book of spells...those of magic-users must be spoken or read aloud."[91] Dr. John Eric Holmes, the editor of D&D said, "The level of violence in this make-believe world runs high. There is hardly a game in which the players do not indulge in murder, arson, torture, rape, or highway robbery."[92] The Pokémon card game has about 150 characters on its cards. Each Pokémon has its own special fighting abilities and as a character wins battles its power becomes stronger. Apparently, each species has and releases supernatural powers against each other.

Magic the Gathering is a game where players cast spells on each other as they seek to increase the size of their decks and kill their enemies. There are five types of magic that players can use. Black magic represents the magic of death. Blue magic is artifice, illusion, and deception. Green magic is the magic of life. It has a peaceful exterior, but has vast destructive capability. Red magic is the magic of the earth, fire, chaos, and war. It has tendencies that are also destructive. White magic is spells of healing and protection.

Here are some examples of "Magic the Gathering" cards: the "Ley Druid" is a summon cleric card. (1)The card says, "Untap a land of your choice." This ability is played as an interrupt. After years of training, the Druid becomes one with nature, drawing power from the land and returning it when needed. This card gives some basics of Wiccanism. (2) The "Spitting Earth" card is a sorcery card that says, "spitting earth deals to target creature an amount of damage

---

[91] Gary Gygax, <u>Advanced Dungeons and Dragons Handbook</u>, 1st Edition, (Lake Geneva, WI: TSR, 1987) p.25.
[92] John Eric Holmes, "Confessions of a Dungeon Master," <u>Psychology Today</u> November 1980.

equal to the number of mountains you control. There are times solid ground gives precious little comfort." Sorcery is used in many occultic circles and is an abomination in the Bible. (3) The "Initiates of the Ebon Hand" is a summons cleric card and it says, "Many Initiates sacrificed a hand to become full members of the Order."

Each summons cleric card has a shaman, witch, or a Druid Pagan priest practicing some form of witchcraft. (4) The "Shamite Healer" card is also known as a summons cleric card and it says, "Prevent 1 damage to any creature or player. Healers ultimately acquire the divine gifts of spiritual and physical wholeness. The most devout are also granted the ability to pass physical wholeness on to others." The shaman is actually mixing up occultic potions on the card. (5) The "Wall of Bone" card is a "Summon Wall" card and it says, "The wall of bone is said to be an aspect of the Great Wall in Hel, where the bones of all sinners wait for Ragnarok, when Hela will call them forth for the final battle." This card gives an occultic view of what Hell will be like on the Judgment Day of Jesus' return. Most occultists believe the opposite of what Christians believe.

Georgia Pabst of the Milwaukee Journal Sentinel says, "Magic the Gathering" takes place in the mystical multi-universe of Dominia, where players become mighty wizards and armed with beautifully illustrated cards of various creatures, artifacts and lands, cast spells and enchantment aimed at killing of the opponent."[93]

So, basically each game teaches the players to assume the role of someone using magical spells, etc. over and over

[93] Georgia Pabst, "Success of Fantasy Sci-fi Card Games is Magical," <u>Milwaukee Journal Sentinel</u>, 6 August 1995.

and over again. Some of the questions I've heard over the years sound like this, "But it's just a game. That magic isn't real, is it?"

Actually, the witchcraft taught in each of these games, especially D&D and Magic the Gathering, are very much like practicing some forms of witchcraft, such as hermetic magic. While true, it is not like practicing "ceremonial magic," but it is just like some forms of witchcraft.

Wizards of the Coast target-marketed its games, which we just described, to 3 to 16-year-olds. However, many people much older do play. "Wizards of the Coast also spent 7 million dollars to advertise 'Duel Masters,' which has these very same concepts, on Cartoon Network and has advertised on public schools milk cartons and

posters. They released 325 units in schools in 21 major markets to reach 6 million U.S. students a day."[94]

It is my experience, from working with 4500 teenagers over 7 years, that those children who have been involved with some from of FRPG can and do become affected by them, in one degree, or another.

What is happening is that the children put to practice in real life what they learned from the FRPG. This is an all too common thing in our culture. This is a quote by an ex-Satanist named Sean Sellers about his involvement in D&D. "After I became a Satanist, I used D&D manuals for their magical symbols and character references for my initial studies. I also used my experience as a Dungeon master to

---

[94] Damon White, "Breakfast with Duel Masters," Gaming Report, Article on "GAMA" trade show, 15 March 2005, p.1.

introduce people to satanic behavior concepts and recruit them into the occult."[95]

When I lived on the streets in Atlanta, GA, I had friends who were in the occult and some were Satanists. They would recruit people who were into things like FRPG's into their organizations.

The argument that FRPGs are not dangerous just isn't true! My experience working with over 4500 teenagers is the same as those facts we looked at previously. FRPGs can and sometimes do open the door to some type of occultism in many cases.

One Halloween I was preparing to give a television presentation and obtained a few Yu-Gi-Oh cards from a teenager to use during the presentation. I was in a hurry and stuck the cards in my laptop case without praying over the cards to break their power. That night my wife woke up and started praying. She started rebuking a spirit of witchcraft. She started to pray and the Holy Spirit told her that a spirit of witchcraft was open because of something called Yu-Gi-Oh. My wife had never even heard of the cards and I didn't tell her that the cards were brought into the house. She had no idea they were in the house. She told me the next morning what had happened and I immediately prayed over the cards and told her what the cards were and that they were in the house. That clearly proves the ability for a "harmless" FPRG to open up a door to witchcraft.

Let's look at the characteristics of games like: D&D, Magic the Gathering, Duel Masters, and Yu-Gi-Oh. The number one primary focus has to do with some form of occultism. Number two; the games are either violent and/or

---

[95] Micheal Stackpole, The Pulling Report, 1990: p.40.

manipulative in nature. Number three; they are very addictive. Magic the Gathering has often been called by its players "Magic the Addicting" or "Magic the Disease." Number four; the players identify with the behavior of the character over and over again, soon internalizing the behaviors. Number five; FPRGs do saturate an anti-God worldview.

INCIDENTS FROM INVOLVEMENT

People ask me all the time things like, "Has there ever been anyone who has really been affected by these games?" Yes, there have been and still are many. I have personally counseled two teenagers that were severely oppressed by demonic forces after playing the fantasy role playing game "Final Fantasy." The quote we read earlier by Sean Sellers was after he had been convicted for killing three people in 1987, two of whom were his parents. Sean admitted his interest in the occult began with D&D. Just in the 1980's and early 90's have we documented twelve cases in which either suicides or murders took place by hardcore players of D&D alone. One man who went on an eight state crime spree including murder, quoted to the Detroit Free Press, "Have you ever heard of D&D? That had a lot to do with it… It is not just a board game. It's a lot deeper than a board game. I've got five friends that are locked up for the same thing (murder) right now because of the game." Timothy Grice from Lafayette, CO committed suicide by a shotgun blast in 1983. On his police report, the detective's note says, "D&D became a reality. He thought he was not constrained to this life, but could leave it and return because of the game."[96] Many of today's FRPGs were based on the same concepts as D&D. So, there's no difference in the effects that the concepts can have on the player.

A psychologist by the name of Dr. Craig A. Anderson did a study on the effects of violent video games on thoughts, feeling, and behavior. He suggests that video games, because they are engrossing and require the player to identify with the character, are more harmful than watching violence on television or in movies.[97] If the content changes to occultic material, the concepts stay the same, then the person will be affected by occultism instead of violence.

A WORD FROM THE WORD

The rebuttal I get to my argument is, "Well, I have friends who play Magic the Gathering and Duel Masters and they don't practice witchcraft or have very many problems. They are even Christians." First, I would ask you, how long have they been playing? The effect of occultic propaganda usually doesn't happen overnight. It usually takes place over time, undetected and very deceptive. But, for the sake of argument, let's just say it wasn't affecting them. If they are truly Christian, they must look to the Word of God as their final guideline for truth to determine what is right or wrong.

Like I said earlier, Fantasy Role-Playing Games are saturated with occultic material and concepts. The Bible speaks very clearly about occultism. In Revelation 18:23

---

[96] Yvonne Peterson, Exodus S.A. Occult Program 1987:p.9
[97] C.A. Anderson & K.E. Dill, "Video Games and Aggressive Thoughts, Feelings, and Behavior in the Laboratory and in Life," Journal of Personality and Social Psychology, vol.78, no.4.

(KJV) it says, "for thy (Babylon) merchants were great men of the earth; for by thy sorceries were all nations deceived." This scripture talks about the last day's occultism becoming so wide spread and common that it would be very lucrative worldwide industry that deceives all the nations of the earth. This is very much a description of the gaming industry, the movie industry, and the music industry. It also says in Revelation 21:7-8 (KJV) that "He that overcometh shall inherit all things; and I will be his God and he shall be my son. But the fearful and unbelieving, and the abominable, and murderers, and whoremongers, and sorcerers, and idolaters, and all liars, shall have their parting the lake which burns with fire and brimstone: which is the second death." This scripture puts occultism right up there with murder and all the other evil things mentioned.

The deception comes when you play board games with occultic concepts in them. Over and over again you are internalizing occultic concepts in your mind, which the Bible describes as a part of your soul, which is made up of your mind, will, and emotions. In 2 Corinthians 10:3-5 (KJV) the Bible says, "For though we walk in the flesh, we do not war in the flesh. For the weapons of our warfare are not carnal, but mighty through God to the pulling down of strongholds; Casting down imaginations, and every high thing that exalteth itself against the knowledge of God, and bringing into captivity every thought to the obedience of Christ."

As Christians we should be meditating on things that will reinforce and build up our relationship with Jesus Christ, not the occultic propaganda in FRPGs, occultic music, and ungodly movies.

The good news is that the blood of Jesus Christ has the power to transform your life and the Bible can transform your mind. There are many Christian Fantasy games, as well. Whatever games you play, make sure you analyze the central story theme for content, and see if it is contrary to your faith.

Chapter 9
BEHIND THE DOORS OF DIVINATION: ASTROLOGY

WHAT'S YOUR SIGN?

If I were to walk into a crowd and ask the average person, "What is divination?" most people wouldn't know what I was talking about, but if I were to walk into the same crowd and ask, "What is your sign?" 90% of the people would tell me what their astrological sign or Zodiac sign would be.

Today there are many forms of divination being practiced. We will attempt to briefly cover them. I want to focus on the most commonly practiced and overlooked form in America today, Astrology! Have you ever been outside on a hot summer's night in a place where there is no light, just clear open sky? It is absolutely phenomenal! There is something powerful about staring at the stars. As a young man, I could sit for hours mesmerized by their beauty, but is there something more to the stars than just beauty?

"In America, one out of every four people believes in Astrology. There are ten million devoted followers and 40 million followers who dabble in Astrology in the USA. There are 1200 full time Astrologers in the United States along with 175,000 other part time Astrologers. Three out of every four newspapers carry astrological horoscopes. There are about 12,000 newspapers. Two-thirds of the English read Astrology columns along with 53% of the French, and 63% of the Germans. The fastest growing class of believers in Astrology is made up of executives and professionals."[98] You can hear about it on talk shows, in department stores, in drug stores, in bus and train stations. Over 200 college campuses have 24-hour horoscope computer services. Kids can find Astrology in coloring books, on cereal boxes, on Barbie dolls, and it can even be in the comic strips. Many people will not go to work in the morning unless they have read their horoscopes in the paper. Tabloids are full of the predictions of psychics and astrologers. I was surfing the Internet just recently and saw a pop-up that said, "Find out if he's the one for you. Get an accurate Astrology reading."

But what is Astrology? Where did Astrology come from? What does the Bible say about Astrology? What are the facts about Astrology? Is it okay for a Christian to follow their horoscopes or is it just another form of occultism?

---

[98] <u>Roper Starch Worldwide Survey Report</u>, Conde Nast Publications, 1996.

THE HISTORY

The word "astrology" comes from two Greek words: "astra," meaning "star" and "logos," meaning "word." It refers to "words of the stars." If someone is following Astrology, they are following the words of the stars. The Webster's dictionary defines Astrology as, "The divination of the supposed influences of the stars and the planets on human affairs and terrestrial events by their positions and aspects."[99] In Astrology, there are 12 Zodiac signs or sun signs, which are as follows: Aries, Taurus, Gemini, Cancer, Leo, Virgo, Libra, Scorpio, Sagittarius, Capricorn, Aquarius, and Pisces. In Astrology, there are four elements: fire, earth, air, and water. Each Zodiac or sun sign has positive or negative qualities known by the names Yang and Yin. Each Zodiac sign will fall into an element category.

Each Zodiac sign must also have a ruler, for example: Mars is Aries' ruler and The Sun is Leo's ruler. There are many different types of Astrology such as: Electional Astrology, Horary Astrology, Side Real Astrology, Medical Astrology, Political Astrology, and Mundane Astrology.

Astrology, as generally understood, is the picking of favorable times for doing things, the answering of questions, the forecasting of events, and the analysis of one's destiny, all based on an Astrology chart. The chart has a particular degree or sign that is marked as the beginning point of the forecasting or analysis. In other words, based on where the stars are positioned at birth determines the outcome of your event or destiny. The

---

[99] Webster's New Collegiate Dictionary (Springfield, Massachusetts: G&C Merriam Co., 1979) p.69.

planets, phases of the moon, and stellar positions are all factored to determine one's sign and characteristics.

People, who are devoted followers of Astrology, look to their astrological horoscopes for "divine" insight into life's situations and circumstances. People have been doing this for thousands of years and all the way up to now. You might be familiar with famous Astrologers like Jeanne Dixon, Carol Righter, Snyder Omar, and Francis Drake, but did you know that Astrology dates back all the way to 4,000 BC?

The first historical evidence of people practicing Astrology for guidance was in Mesopotamia, or Modern day Iraq. This area is known as the "cradle" of civilization in which all the races and peoples of the earth, as we know it, originated. Over the period of 4,000 BC to 30 BC, many different people conquered this area, e.g.: The Ubaidians, Sumerians, Akkadians, Babylonians, Assyrians, Parthians, Persians, and more.

During all these changes of power of kingdoms, the people intermarried cultures. In doing so, the practice of Astrology continued to thrive beyond its original cultural boundaries. Up until 300 years ago, Astrology and Astronomy were considered the same and known as Astrologia. The study of Astronomy is the study of the stars and planets for scientific purposes, while Astrology remains a source of divine predictions from the stars. Astrology was first for kings. All the courts of Europe had official Astrologers. They sought guidance for their ruler through the stars. "The first popular horoscopes for the masses were published in 1493 as an almanac called "The Kalendar and Compost of Shepards." In 1930, the London Sunday Express published an astrological article on the birth of

Princess Margaret. The public response was phenomenal, leading to a commission for an Astrologer to write a series column. Circulation was incredible and newspapers in England, Germany, France, and America began publishing columns of astrological predictions, and that was the beginning of mass Astrology as we know it today."[100]

While it is a fact that Astrology has been around as long as mankind and our culture is completely saturated with its influence, is Astrology a harmless observation of the stars or is there something more behind the movement?

Alester Crowley, the father of modern Satanism, was a follower of Astrology. He, like most Astrologers, believed that the earth is in an astrological time period called "the Age of Aquarius." The Age of Aquarius is an astrological time period, which was believed to have started in the early 1900's. Alester Crowley and his followers claim that this period is a time when there is a heightened spiritual awareness in the earth and that during this time is when the spirit of Hours or Anti-Christ will be released on earth.

Alester Crowley, announced that, Sybil Leek, a world renowned Astrologer, British witch, and occult scholar, who also authored four books on Astrology, would someday pick up where Crowley would leave off in occultism. The last time Leek saw him was in 1947, shortly before his death.[101]

---

[100] Jim Tester, <u>The History of Western Astrology</u>, (Boydell and Brewer, Inc., 1987) p.256.
[101] David Benoit, <u>14 Things Witches Hope Parents Never Find Out</u>, (1994) p.30-32.

THE TIES

There are many ties from Astrology to witchcraft. In the Encyclopedia of Witches and Witchcraft by Rosemary Ellen Guiley, she was quoted as saying "Astrology is perhaps the oldest system of divination and prophecy. Astrology is based on the Hermetic belief that the physical world is a reflection of the cosmos (as above, so below). In Astrology, the positions of the planets, sun, and moon in the Zodiac constellations exert influences on the lives of mankind and the world below. As a complex art, Astrology is used by some modern witches as a divinatory and spiritual development tool."[102]

Another connection of Astrology and witchcraft is found in a USA Today article written about a school of witchcraft in Austria. The founder of the school said in reference to the classes, "Sure, it may sound esoteric, but the class actually focuses on the basics of meteorology, astronomy, and astrology. The studies help students get in touch with their subconscious and recognize and follow intuitions by finding and channeling sources of energy in nature."[103]

In witchcraft, the magic circle provides a sacred and purified space in which all rites, magical work, and ceremonies are conducted. It offers a boundary for a reservoir of consecrated power and acts as a doorway to the "world of gods". The circle symbolizes wholeness, perfection, and unity; the creation of the cosmos; the womb of Mother Earth; and the cycle of the seasons; and birth-death-regeneration. Within the circle, Astrologers believe it

---

[102] Guiely, p.167.
[103] W.E. Vine, p.61

becomes possible to transcend the physical, to open the mind to deeper and higher levels of consciousness. According to Rosemary Ellen Guiely, "The witch works within a magic circle and uses four primary magical tools, which correspond to the elements: fire, earth, water, and air."[104]

Each source, just quoted, was from pro-astrology supporters and the latter two were pro-witchcraft supporters. Each has the same structure and elements for their release of power. The similarities are incredible!

BRINGING IT BACK TO THE BIBLE

The Biblical definition of "divination" is "seeking after the will of the gods, in effort to learn their future action or divine blessing on some proposed future action. Divination was one of man's attempts to know and control the world and the future, apart from the true God. It was the opposite of true prophecy, which essentially is submission to God's sovereignty.

Divination was practiced many different ways in the Bible. It might involve a sacrifice to the deity on an altar, the use of a hole in the ground, through which the diviner spoke to the spirits of the dead. A diviner might shake arrows, consult with household idols, or study the livers of dead animals. No matter how it was done, divination was seeking power, insight, and blessing from anything other than the one true God, Yahweh.

Deuteronomy 4:19 says, "And lest thou lift up thine eyes unto heaven, and when thou seest the sun, and the moon, and the stars, even all the host of heaven, shouldest

---

[104] Freydkin, p.2C

be driven to worship them, and serve them, which the Lord thy God hath divided unto all nations under the whole heaven." It also says in Deuteronomy 18:10-12, "There shall not be found among you any one that maketh his son or his daughter to pass through fire, or that useth divination, or an observer of times (Astrology), or an enchanter, or a witch, or a charmer, or a consulter with familiar spirits, or a wizard, or a necromancer. For all that do these things are an abomination unto the Lord: and because of these abominations the Lord thy God doth drive them out from before thee. Thou shalt be perfect with the Lord thy God. For these nations, which thou shalt possess, hearkened unto observers of times (Astrology), and unto diviners, but as for thee, the Lord thy God hath not suffered thee so to do." God makes it very clear in the Bible how He feels about practices like Astrology and what happens to nations and people who continue to practice those crafts.

You might say, "But it is not like I'm sacrificing to another god or something like they did in the Old Testament. Is it still a sin?" Yes, although today there are many forms of modern divination like: tarot cards, Quija boards, crystal balls, reading palms, or tea leaves, they are all doors of divination.

Astrology is the most common, widespread, deceptive, and overlooked form of divination because many people do it without really understanding what they are doing. One who seeks direction, divine blessing, or guidance from any deity other than the Holy Spirit is practicing divination.

The good news is that the blood of Jesus has redeemed us from the curses that come from practicing any form of witchcraft, especially Astrology. Listen to this passage of scripture in Revelation 1:4-6 (KJV), "…Grace be unto you, and peace, from Him which is, and which was, and which is to come; and from the seven Spirits which are before His throne; And from Jesus Christ, who is the faithful witness, and the first begotten of the dead, and the prince of the kings of the earth. Unto Him that loved us, and washed us from our sins in his own blood, and hath made us kings and priest unto God and his Father, to him be glory and dominion for ever and ever. Amen." The Blood of Jesus makes us sons and daughters of the Most High.

John 16:13-15 says, "...when He, the Spirit of truth, has come, He will guide you into all truth: for He will not speak on His own authority, but whatever He hears He will speak; and He will tell you things to come. He will glorify Me, for He will take of what is Mine and declare it to you. All things that the Father has are Mine. Therefore I said that He will take of Mine and declare it to you." The Holy Spirit, which lives inside you, will guide your life. When you are filled with the Holy Spirit of God, you don't need anything like Astrology to guide you, because you have the Promise from God that He will!

Chapter 10
EXPOSING THE FACES OF HORROR FILMS

INFORMING THE AUDIENCE

Horror films have been a part of American culture since the early 1900's, but in the past few decades, they have become a very hot topic. Exploding in the millennium, horror movies, such as: Freddy Vs. Jason, Dawn of the Dead, Van Helsing, Exorcist: The Beginning, The Grudge, and The Saw 1 & 2 have all been very hot items at the box office. The Grudge took in 70.7 million in 2004 and The Saw grossed over 18 million at the box office.[105] Based on the results of the American consumer, horror is hot and hasn't cooled off in a long time.

But what exactly is a horror film? A horror film is a movie dominated by elements of horror. This cinematic genre incorporates a number of sub-genres and repeated

---

[105] John Hamann, "Box Office Prophets," Box Office Report, 7 May 2005.

themes, including but not limited to slashers, vampires, zombies, demonic possession, Satanism, alien mind control, evil children, cannibalism, werewolves, animals attacking humans, and haunted houses. The horror film is also associated with low budgets and exploitation, but major studios and well-respected directors have made intermittent forays into horror. Many horror films incorporate things like science fiction, as well. Horror is defined as, "A painful and intense fear, dread, or dismay…calculated to inspire feelings of dread or horror."[106]

Many horror films have had so much success consistently that they inspire many sequels, remakes, and copycats. Some movies that apply are: "The Exorcist, Amityville, Silence of the Lambs, Friday 13th, Nightmare on Elm Street, The Saw" and many others. Usually, during the Halloween season, there is an increase in the release of horror films because of their wide success. Horror films have become a billion dollar a year entertainment industry in America captivating audiences with some of the most horrifying and frightening scenes they will ever see in their entire lives. For years I was afraid to go swimming in a pool after watching the movie "Jaws." But even as scared as I was watching it, it was still one of my favorite movies of all time as a child. I recently asked a group of teenagers about their horror film experiences. The average age when they saw their first horror film was 7 years old. They all said that it was the thrill and fear that the movie brought to them emotionally that kept them coming back for more.

As a whole, America is fascinated with entertainment like this. I think about a song that was popular in the 90's

---

[106] Webster's New Collegiate Dictionary, p.547.

by a band called "Nirvana" that adequately describes American culture. In the song called "Smells like Teen Spirit," Kurt Cobain was quoted as saying, "Here we are now, entertain us." But what exactly is entertainment like this doing to our society? Is it entertainment or a little something more? Where did the "horror film industry" come from?

The first horror film ever created was a vampire flick by the name of "Le Manior du Diable" directed by George Melies in 1896. It was only two minutes long, but audiences loved it. In 1922, German director, F.W. Murnaus, released the first full-length vampire feature, "Nosferatu". Later that next year, the Hollywood favorite, "The Hunchback of Notre Dame," was released with America's first horror film movie star, Lon Chaney. Soon to follow in the 30's were films like "Dracula", "Frankenstein", and "The Mummy", which were released by Universal Studios, bringing to the screen a series of successful Gothic-steeped features. Then the 50's saw a shift from Gothic toward Modern. Aliens crept into horror with films like "The Thing from Another World" and "Invasion of the Body Snatchers." The 60's introduced the classic horror film "Psycho." In the 70's, public fascination with the occult was higher than ever. This led to great success of many series of supernatural themed, often explicitly gruesome horror movies, two of the most successful being "The Exorcist" and "The Omen."

The trend was set for decades in the horror film industry that produced movies like "Halloween," "Friday 13th," "Scream," and "The Blair Witch Project." And now in the 2000's that same trend hasn't changed much, giving us the ability to define horror elements and themes fairly consistently.

In this millennia, films like "Dawn of the Dead", which is filled with all the common traits of a successful horror film, not only are sweeping the cinemas, but the DVD sales are setting all time records. Another film is "The Saw" and is all about a jig saw killer, who puts people that are dissatisfied with their lives into positions to choose to die, or do something crazy to live. The only person that survived any of the killer's schemes was a woman, who had a reverse bear trap in her mouth. In 24 hours it would go off and do fatal damage to her head. The only way out of the trap was to get the key out of a man's intestines after he ingested the key. She had to actually do this or she would die, which she did. By the end of the movie, everyone died except this woman and the killer got away with every single murder. This movie grossed over 18 million at the box office. The description of this movie was given to me first by a group of teenage boys from the ages 13-14. They were telling me that they were fascinated by this movie and it was one of their favorite films of all time.

IMPACTING OUR CULTURE

What kind of impact is horror having on our culture? Is all this just a bunch of harmless entertainment or are all the monsters, killers, devils, and vampires having negative impact on our nation? A very well known psychologist, Dr. Craig A. Anderson, did a study on the effects of violent music and violent video games on children, college age, and adults. The study found that a typical child in the U.S. watches 28 hours of TV weekly, seeing as many as 8,000 murders by the time he or she finishes elementary school at age 11. Even worse, the killers are depicted as getting away with the murders 75% of the time while showing no remorse or accountability. He said "Such TV violence socialization may make children immune to brutality and aggression, while others become fearful of living in such a dangerous society." Dr. Anderson said, "One major conclusion from this and other research on violent entertainment media is that content matters, but especially for parents of children and adolescents."[107]

A study done by the Surgeon General's Scientific Advisory Committee on Television and Social Behavior, formed in 1969 to access the impact of violence on the attitudes, values, and behaviors of viewers, found that children may become less sensitive to the pain and suffering of others, children may be more fearful of the world around them, and they may be more likely to behave in aggressive or harmful ways toward others."[108]

If these studies showed violence causes these children and college age to have violent behaviors, then what about the effects of scary media? There was a study done in 1998 in Ohio that revealed growing evidence that violence viewed can cause fears and anxieties in young viewers. For example, 2,000 third through eighth graders were surveyed and the study revealed that as the number of hours of television viewing increased, so did the prevalence of symptoms of psychological trauma, such as anxiety, depression, and post-traumatic stress. Another study in 1999 surveyed parents of almost 500 Rhode Island children in kindergarten through fourth grade. It revealed that the amount of children's television viewing, especially at bedtime, and having a TV on in one's own bedroom was

---

[107] Anderson & Dill, vol. 78, no.4
[108] Anderson & Dill, vol.78, no.4

significantly related to the frequency of sleep disturbances. 9% of the parents' surveys reported that their child experienced TV-induced nightmares at least once a week. 62% of parents with children between the ages of 2 and 17 reported that their children had been frightened by something they saw on a TV program or movie. Two independent studies of adults showed reports of having been frightened by a TV show or movie and demonstrated that the presence of vivid, detailed memories of enduring media-induced fear is nearly universal. A study done on University of Wisconsin and University of Michigan students, reported disturbances in the sleep of 52%, mental preoccupation with disturbing material in 22%, and 35% reported dreading or avoiding the situation depicted in the movie. One fourth of the respondents said that the impact of the program or movie (viewed an average of six years earlier) was still with them at the time of reporting.[109] In other words, 25% had an experience just like the incident I had as a child with the movie Jaws and the fear of swimming. The facts are that horror films can and do affect people, especially younger children, with fears, anxieties, and sleep disturbances.

Can the witchcraft, violence, and satanic propaganda in horror films really affect you spiritually? Are there Satanists in the horror films industry? What does the Bible say about horror films?

---

[109] M.I. Singer, K. Slovak, T. Frierson, & P. York, "Viewing Preferences Symptoms of Psychological Trauma, and Violent Behaviors Among Children Who Watch TV," Journal of the American Academy of Child and Adolescent Psychiatry, (1998) 37: p.1041-1048.

NOW SHOWING: SPIRITUAL RELEVANCE

As we talked about earlier, the horror film industry has a set trend that frequently has themes of witchcraft and Satanism in them, but can they really affect you? "The Devil's Advocate" was a film with actor Al Paccino starring as the devil in a lawyer's role and Keanu Reeves as a young inspiring lawyer who was eventually faced with a choice of "selling his soul" and working for the law firm to get guilty people, some of whom practiced witchcraft, off the hook. The movie has some scenes of voodoo rituals, but was not nearly as detailed and graphic as most movies today.

Some people might say, "Oh, it's just a movie, it can't hurt you spiritually." But when I saw that movie I was struggling with spiritual truth and after watching the movie, it did affect my choices. If, as the research showed, violent content causes violent behaviors and fearful content causes nightmares, fear, and anxiety, one can only conclude that a spiritual desensitization will also take place just like it did with me. Like Dr. Anderson said earlier in conclusion of his studies, "Content matters." Satanists know this is true and are actually teaching satanic concepts through movie themes to propagate their message and to ingrain these concepts in today's youth.

THEIR AGENDA

A priest in the Church of Satan, Rex Nichols, stated on a video program called, "They Sold Their Souls to Rock-N-Roll" that the Church of Satan is doing this on all scales, which include, movies, music, art, etc. They call this concept "aesthetic terrorism." Anton Levey, the founder of the Church of Satan, and the author of the Satanic Bible said, "Let's give me a little credit for having moved society up or down, but for at least having moved it." He went on to say that all satanic Rock lyrics, satanic movies, even satanic murders are all stepchildren from his Church of Satan.[110] There are movies and music production companies with the sole purpose of creating products to desensitize you to the message and concepts that the Church of Satan teaches. Examples include: Devil Music, Inc., which owns the rights to "System of a Down's" lyrics. This is just one example of 100's of companies out there. If the process didn't work to some degree, the Church of Satan would not use it.

Rob Zombie, who is a Satanist, had been creating satanic music for years. Just a few years ago he started making horror films. One is called, "House of 1,000 Corpses" and has a sequel to it called, "The Devil's Rejects". He openly admitted on a TV show called "Uranium" that it does desensitize people to the message and that he is getting very rich off the de- and re-programming of satanic material through horror films. It's very obvious, based on these facts, how horror films can affect your mind. Medically, we have looked at how the occult uses these avenues. But, what does the Bible say about horror films? What is happening is that people are becoming "interested" in what they are seeing and start to become seduced into experimenting with witchcraft and Satanism. The Bible says in I Timothy 4:1 (KJV), "Now the Spirit speaketh expressly, that in the latter times some shall depart from the faith, giving heed to seducing spirits, and doctrines of devils." The Greek word for "doctrines" here is

---

[110] They Sold Their Souls for Rock-N-Roll, videocassette, Fight the Good Fight Ministries, 2001 (240 min.)

interpreted as "instruction, the function, the information, learning, or teachings."[111]

In other words, in the last days before Christ returns some people will leave a Christian faith and turn to Satanic concepts through an avenue that shares, distributes, and teaches their concepts. The number one way that this is happening right now is through today's mainstream media and horror films.

WHATSOEVER THINGS ARE TRUE

What does the Bible say to do to combat teachings and propaganda like this? The Apostle Paul gave us a very good prescription to win the battle in your mind. In Philippians 4:8 (KJV) he says, "Finally, brethren, whatsoever things are true, whatsoever things are honest, whatsoever things are just, whatsoever things are pure, whatsoever things are lovely, whatsoever things are of good report; if there be any virtue, and if there be any praise, think on these things." The bottom line is whatever you are putting into your mind will affect your spirit as well as your soul, which is your mind. I used this same principle as I was breaking away from the occult and drug addiction. Occultic oppression, drug addiction, and the crazy thoughts that come from both dominated my mind for seven years. After I received Jesus as my Savior and asked the Holy Spirit to live in my heart, I started reading the Bible. Every time overpowering thoughts would come, I would break out this dusty old Bible I had found and I would read it, sometimes aloud. Every time these thoughts would try to conquer my life, I

---

[111] James Strong, <u>The New Strong's Exhaustive Concordance of the Bible</u> (Nashville, TN: Thomas Nelson Publishers, 1990) p.23

combated them with the Scriptures. The thoughts and demonic oppression would go away. The change was so powerful that it changed my life forever. I wrote a book called, "Warring with the Word," which gives detailed accounts of these events and the victory I obtained by reading God's Word.

You might be asking, "But what do we do to get started? I mean I've watched a lot of things that are still tattooed in my mind?"

First of all, you must repent for your part in allowing yourself to meditate or think on evil things, and then renounce those things. Next, don't do them anymore, receive the blood of Jesus over those sins and ask the Holy Spirit to empower you for victory. Understand that the battlefield is in your mind. Your mind must be renewed on a constant basis with the Word of God. You quickly find out that the Bible is a lot more exciting and interesting than a horror flick. Don't take my word for it. Try it for yourself!

Chapter 11
SYMBOLS IN AMERICAN CULTURE

SCRIBBLES, SQUIGGLES, AND SYMBOLS

What are symbols, amulets, and talismans and what is really behind some of the symbols in America's culture? Some of you might be saying, what is an amulet or talisman? And what's wrong with symbols? In this chapter, we are going to look at some very popular symbols that you've probably seen on a CD cover, or in a movie, or on a t-shirt. These symbols we are going to talk about are very commonly found on jewelry and stickers, as well. Because of media and different cultural fads and trends, the meanings of most of these symbols are usually not understood by consumers. Think about it, if you have ever been to a Rock concert, you've seen necklaces, bracelets, bags, shirts, stickers, all with various types of symbols and writing on them. Even the backdrops that bands use often contain some type of symbol on them.

I was recently watching the "Live 8" fundraiser for the African nations on MTV. Madonna came out on stage to perform. The backdrop she used was full of what appeared to be Hebrew writings. Millions of people watched as she sang a song called "Like a Prayer". What were the symbols in the background? Madonna is a self-proclaimed follower of the oldest occultic religion known to man, Kabala.[112] Lots of those people didn't have a clue what those symbols meant. They where just caught up in the moment.

EVERYDAY SYMBOLS

The next time you go into a shirt shop, count how many different symbols on the shirts that you don't recognize or know the meaning. When I first started studying music and the artists of our day, one of the first things I noticed were all the scribbles, squiggles, and symbols found on CD's and covers. Most people, just like I used to be, don't have a clue about the real meaning behind most of our cultural symbols.

If you look at the jewelry that people wear, a large percentage has on it some type of symbol with a meaning. In 2003, $53.6 billion was spent on jewelry, $60 million on music, and several billion dollars in the movie, sticker, magazine, and shirt industry. Additionally, way over half of the products are labeled with some form of symbols. You might be asking, "What's the big deal?" When you get into the history and meaning of symbols, you will quickly find just how big a deal it can be.

From the earliest facts that we have about human culture until now, man has always had symbols to identify

---

[112] Derdre Donahue, "Madonna's Children's Book Rocks the World Market," USA Today, Life Section, 15 September 2003, p.1D.

himself with some aspect of his culture. The oldest mummy we have, which is the Ice Age mummy, had tattoos to symbolize aspects of his culture and to this day 95% of all tattoos symbolize something to the individual that receives them.

Many of what we call symbols today, whether charms or on jewelry, have been known for centuries as talismans and amulets. A talisman is a charm, which has magical, empowering abilities or powers of their own, which is transmitted to their possessors. Most are used to attract good luck and to ward off evil. An amulet is very similar to a talisman. Amulets are magical objects typically marked with symbols believed to attract good or repel evil, depending on the purpose. There is a long tradition throughout history that talismans and amulets are made by alchemists, shamans, witches, and priests. They are sold or given to the public. When they are made they are usually "blessed" in some form of ritual ceremony. In other words, when these objects are bought, or given to their possessor, the object is active and bestows the magical power to the possessor. Many talismans and amulets have precious, even rare, gemstones in them, which are believed to possess magical power endowed by nature.

IN THE PAST

The Egyptians and Babylonians used them when attempting to alter the forces of nature. The Egyptian word for amulet is "mk-t" which means "protection." The most powerful Egyptian objects were those that were inscribed with the names of gods. One example is the "scarab," which is the symbol for the Egyptian god of creation. The scarab frequently was put on the dead to affect their resurrection.

Some were placed in mummy's hands or under their necks. The purpose of the amulets was usually the determining factor of where on the mummy it was placed. Another amulet was the frog. It was the symbol of the Egyptian god of fertility and was usually made of gold. Two features on the head represent the sun god Ra and the god Osiris.

In ancient African culture, the carrying of an animal's foot or other parts of a swift creature were supposed to help a person be able to escape or flee with the speed of an animal. The "lucky rabbit's foot" charm was handed down and incorporated into our culture by enslaved Africans, who were brought to the New World. The Mojo bag was also borrowed from centuries of African voodoo ceremonies and incorporated into our American culture. The idea is that certain items (spices, teeth, feathers) placed in a bag and "blessed" would produce a magical effect for that person who carries it.

In Eastern Europe, during the Middle Ages, legends of zombies and vampires were prevalent especially during the time of the plague deaths and the time a certain Romanian Prince (Vlad the Impaler), horribly tortured and killed thousands. To ward off such vampires, charms and talismans were employed. Legend had it that zombies and vampires couldn't attack you if you held up a cross in their faces, threw holy water on them, or wore a chain of garlic around your neck.[113]

---

[113] Danial Stolzenburg, The Study of Amulets in Modern Europe, Institute for the History of Science

SATANIC SYMBOLS

A.

A. UPRIGHT PENTAGRAM: *Symbolizes the Morning Star, a name that Satan has taken. This symbol is used within witchcraft and in occultic rituals in the conjuration of evil spirits. You are more likely to find this symbol encased within a circle which is believed to confine the power.*

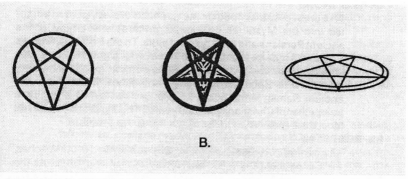

B.

B. INVERTED PENTAGRAM: *When the Pentagram is in this position it represents the he-goat viewed by Satanists as a symbol for Satan. Notice that the top portion of the pentagram actually has the head of a goat within it. Penta, meaning five; Pentagram symbolizes the five-pointed star.*

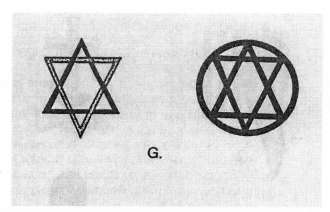

G.

G. HEXAGRAM: *(Also referred to as Solomon's Seal) This symbol was used by the Egyptians long before the Israeli's adopted it as their own. The Jews began using the Star of David during their Babylonian captivity and it, of course, now has a definite Jewish meaning that cannot be condemned. The Hexagram is also used in the occult, astrology, and in various rituals. It is the root word from which we coined the phrase "to put a hex on something or someone."*

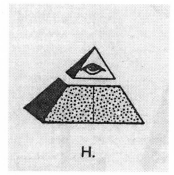

H.

H. THE ILLUMINATED EYE: *This symbol originally represented "the eye of Hours," the Sun God. Its meaning today reportedly stands for the Illuminatti (which is interpreted as Bearers of the Light, Lucifer, whose name means "Bringer of the Light.")The Illuminatti is a world-wide council that controls the occult in all of its forms. When placed above the pyramid as the capstone, it represents their watchful eye over all the earth.*

I. THE BROKEN 'S' OR SATANIC 'S': *The Satanic 'S' represents a thunderbolt and means "destroyer." In mythology it was the weapon of Zeus. This medallion is worn to give power over others. You may remember that this symbol was worn by the soldiers of Nazi Germany.*

K. BROKEN CROSS: *It is a mockery of the cross of Jesus Christ. A person joining Satanism may, in ritual, be handed a ceramic cross to invert and break down the cross bars in order to show rejection of Christ. This symbol came out of the Dark Ages.*

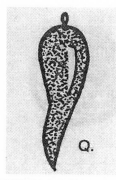

Q. ITALIAN HORN, UNICORN HORN, OR LEPRICHAUN STAFF: *It is used to ward off "maluka" or the "evil eye." It also means that Satan will take care of your finances.*

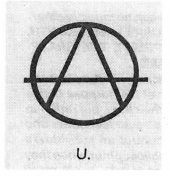

U. ANARCHY: *This is the symbol of anarchy. It was first widely used by "Punk Rockers and Thrashers." It is now used heavily by Heavy, Black, and Speed Rockers. It represents a total rebellion against all authority and the abolishment of all law.*

W.

W. SIX SIX SIX (666): *The number of the Beast (Satan, Anti-Christ). In the last book of the Bible, Revelation 13:18, it states, "Let him that has understanding count the number of the Beast; for it is the number of a man; and his number is six hundred, three score and six (666)."*

Y.

Y. HORNED HAND (SATANIC SALUTE): *The "Horned Hand" is the sign of recognition between those who are in the occult. It may also innocently be used by those who identify with heavy metal music.*

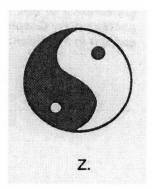

Z.

Z. YIN-YANG: *In Chinese philosophy, there are two great opposite principles or forces on whose interplay everything in the universe depends. Yang is male, light and positive. Yin is female, dark and negative. All phenomena can be classified in terms of them.*

BB

BB. GOATHEAD: *The horned god, Goat of Mendes, Baphomet, God of the Witches, the Scapegoat. It is a Satanist's way of mocking Christ as the "Lamb" who died for the sins of humanity.*

CC

CC. SIGNS OF THE ZODIAC: *The Signs of the Zodiac are used in the Satanic or the occultic worship of the gods and goddesses that seek after the lust of Ishtar. Conjuring the spirits of fertility to produce every type of immoral lust after and for the gods of procreation is done through the use of these emblems. The practitioners of the Zodiac are acknowledging their god as Baal, or Lucifer.*

MODERN TIMES

In our modern times, can these charms and talismans, which have been adapted, really have some effect on you even if you are aware or not? I mean, come on, a rabbit's foot? A necklace of garlic to ward off vampires? Just how far fetched is this concept? But in today's culture, what do some of these symbols look like? Are shamans and witches still making these objects of power? And if so, where exactly can we find these symbols?

A lot of symbols used in today's culture are very blatant in their meanings, but for those who don't know, they just don't know. Here are a few examples: The inverted pentagram is very a common symbol in Satanism. When the pentagram is in this position, it represents the he-goat viewed by Satanists as a symbol for Satan. The top portion of the pentagram actually has the head of a goat within it. "Penta" means five. The pentagram symbolizes the five-pointed star.

The upright pentagram symbolizes the "Morning Star," a name that Satan has taken. This symbol is used within witchcraft and in occultic rituals in the conjuration of evil spirits. You are most likely to find this symbol encased within a circle. The ritual circle is believed to confine the power in the occult.[114] Many different bands and organizations put this symbol on their products or music to show their allegiance to the occult. One band for example is the satanic band, Sum 41. The power derived from the pyramid is one of the major powers within the occult and the power is supposedly greater when inverted. This is also symbolic of male deity.[115]

The hexagram, also referred to as Solomon's seal, was used by the Egyptians long before Israel adopted it as their own. The Jews began using it during their Babylonian captivity and it, of course, now has a definite Jewish meaning that cannot be condemned. The Hexagram is also used in the occult, Astrology, and in various other rituals. It is the root word from which we coined the phrase, "to put a hex on something."[116]

The illuminated eye originally represented "the eye of hours," the sun god. Its meaning today reportedly stands for the Illuminati, which is interpreted as "bearers of the light." This is a reference to Lucifer, whose name means "bringer of the light." The Illuminati is a worldwide council that

---

[114] Billy Mayo, <u>Occultic Symbols: What You Don't Know Can Hurt You,</u> p.1A&B.
[115] Billy Mayo, p.1D&E.
[116] Billy Mayo, p.1G

controls the occult in many forms. When placed above the pyramid as the capstone, it represents their watchful eye over all the earth.[117]

The broken "S" or satanic "S" represents a thunderbolt and means destroyer. In mythology it was the weapon of Zeus. The medallion is worn to give power over others. You may remember that this symbol was worn by the Nazi soldiers of Germany and is used by the band "KISS."[118]

Some of these symbols are more commonly used in our culture and would be more easily overlooked in most cases. The Broken Cross or the cross of Nero, which dates back to the 70's, came out as representing "peace." It is really a representation of a mockery of the cross of Jesus Christ.[119] A person joining Satanism may, in ritual, be handed a ceramic cross to invert and break down the cross bars in order to show rejection of Christ. This symbol came out of the Dark Ages and can be found on the satanic band "A Perfect Circle's" album.[120]

The anarchy symbol was first used widely by "punk rockers." It is very common in metal and skating circles. It is an occultic representation that means total rebellion against all authority and the abolishment of all law.[121]

The "horned hand" or the "Cornuto" is also known as the satanic salute. It is a sign of recognition between those who are in the occult. It is also used widely in the music world, representing the followers' identification with the

---

[117] Billy Mayo, p.1H

[118] Billy Mayo, p.2I

[119] Billy Mayo, p.2K

[120] A Perfect Circle, <u>Emotive</u>, compact disc, Spivak Sobol Entertainment, 2004.

[121] Billy Mayo, p.3U

message of the music. Many people use this symbol without realizing its real meaning.[123] If you look very close while the hand is in this shape, three 6's are formed with the fingers.

The six, six, six symbol is used in many different forms and it represents the number of "the beast" (Satan or Anti-Christ), which is talked about in Revelation 13:18.[124] The bass player for the band Audio Slave has this symbol tattooed on his shoulder.

The Yin-Yang is well known in Chinese philosophy. It represents the two great opposite forces on whose interplay everything in the universe depends. Yang is male, light, and positive. Yin is female, dark, and negative.[125]

The signs of the Zodiac are used in the satanic worship of the gods and goddesses that seek after the lust of Ishtar. Conjuring the spirits of fertility to produce every type of immoral lust after and for the gods of procreation is done through the use of these emblems. The practitioners of the Zodiac are acknowledging their god as Baal, or Lucifer.[126]

Are there modern day shamans and witches still doing these things like making talismans with symbols like these on them? Two of the most popular occultic books are The Satanic Bible, written by Anton Levey, the founder of the Church of Satan, and The Necronomicon, written by the American occultic author, Howard Phillips Lovecraft. The Necronomicon has methods of creating these objects and a lot of people are using them. Another group called the "Order of the Golden Dawn," which Alester Crowley and

---

[123] Billy Mayo, p.4Y
[124] Billy Mayo, p.3W
[125] Billy Mayo, p.4Z
[126] Billy Mayo, p.15CC

Davie Bowie, a musician, were a part of specializing in making these talismans and amulets with some of those symbols. There are actually many groups and people that are still practicing this stuff. Before I opened a bar in South Carolina, back in 1996, a high priest in the "Santeria" occult made a talisman with stones. It was suppose to cause the bar to prosper.   In 2001, a book came out called, <u>Making Talismans- Living Entities of Power</u>. It took several different methods from Shamanism, Paganism, and the Order of the Golden Dawn, and mixed them together. The book will "train you in techniques from the simplest to the most complex until you can perform advanced magical talisman operations."[127]

Actually a lot of groups are doing things like this and it seems to be subtle and gaining in popularity, although not understood by the mainstream population. For instance, the Church of Satan claims to practice what is known as "aesthetic terrorism" in America on the youth of our nation.

Aesthetic terrorism is defined by Satanist Rex Nicholson as "the dissemination of 'inform' through the avenues of art, music, movies, books, anyway the information can reach the youth of our nation and most of the time the youth don't understand its effects at first." It's used to propagate the central message of the Church of Satan and make it accepted and interesting.[128]

This push is seen throughout young America culture. You can see this in the skater magazine, "Thrasher," in which some of the symbols for the magazine include: the

---

[127] Nick Farrell, <u>Making Talisman Living Entities of Power</u>, (St.Paul, MN: Llewellyn Publications, 2001.

[128] <u>They Sold Their Souls for Rock-N-Roll</u>, videocassette, Fight the Good Fight Ministries, 2001, (240 min.)

horned god- "Goat of Mendes" and Baphomet- "God of Witches" on their sticker selection.[129] Also the 666 symbol is seen in the magazine and on the bass player for "Audio Slave" and former player of "Rage Against the Machine", which is tattooed on his shoulders and shown in all their CD sleeves and music videos.[130] Some gangs are known to graffiti certain symbols on walls and streets. Then they cast spells within these symbols known as "watchers." The demons released watch the physical blocks of land and if rival gangs or police come they know about it before time.

I used to conduct youth Bible studies at a behavior modification school and a self-styled Satanist used to take pieces of paper, write symbols on the paper, cast evil spells over them, and hide them in our services to spy on us and disrupt us. We really had to pray to break the power of those spells through the blood of Jesus.

You can also see in the satanic punk band, "Sum 41" a hidden pentagram in the band's symbol, which is kind of hidden unless you knew what it was.

In the book, <u>14 Things Witches Hope Parents Never Find Out</u>, by David Benoit, he tells a story about a girl coming up to him after one of his services who was having some demonic activity in her life. When she came up, he noticed an "Italian horn" around her neck. The Italian horn is also called the Unicorn horn and is used in occultism to ward off "maluka," or "the evil eye." It also means Satan will take care of your finances. She said she was having bizarre demonic activity and while he was preaching his

---

[129] "Ten Years of Templeton," <u>Thrasher Magazine</u>, July 2001, Issue 246:p.195.
[130] Audio Slave, <u>Audio Slave</u>, compact disc, Sony Music Entertainment and Interscope Records, 2002, Cover p.10.

message on occultism, the horn would burn her chest sometimes so bad she had to lift it off her chest. He prayed for her and she repented for having it and was set free from its effects.[131]

OPENING DOORS IN OUR LIVES

Just how far could this concept go with advances in technology? I have a friend from Atlanta. When he was a teenager he was playing a video game that was full of occultic concepts and occultic symbols. While he was playing the video game, he claims he had convulsions and became demon possessed. I prayed with him a few years after the incident and he repented. He was delivered from some type of demonic oppression resulting from involvement with this game.

When I was younger, I was dating a girl I had gotten pregnant. She had an abortion and during the abortion her best friend performed a ritual in which she claimed to cast the spirit of this unborn baby into a crystal. After the abortion, she gave me the crystal and told me about the process. One night months later and after I gave my life to Jesus, I was packing to move and I found the crystal. I picked up the crystal and started to think about the things that she said when she gave it to me. All of a sudden, this surge of energy started to shoot up my arm. I dropped the crystal to the floor and started pleading the blood of Jesus. I called someone from the church that I attended for some help. Before I placed the call, the person I was calling received a "word of knowledge," which is when the Holy Spirit gives you knowledge about a situation (I Cor. 14).

---

[131] David Benoit, p.61.

Before I could tell her what the situation was, she told me I was dealing with the spirit of Molech, the god of child sacrifice. I immediately repented for my part in the situation and took authority with the name and blood of Jesus Christ over the spirit of Molech. I threw the crystal out of my home and the spirit of God quickly was ushered back into my home.

This crystal opened a door in my home for demonic activity! Just like all these other examples we have given. In Deuteronomy 18:10-12, the Bible says, "There shall not be found among you any one that maketh his son or daughter to pass through the fire, or that useth divination, or an observer of times, or an enchanter, or a witch, or a charmer, or a consulter with familiar spirits, or a wizard, or a necromancer. For all that do these things are an abomination unto the Lord: and because of these abominations the Lord thy God doth drive them out from before thee."

God specifically warns us about these practices and charmers that were in the midst of them. A charmer makes these objects. I was saved, but because I violated God's law, this spirit could still oppress me. If you are not saved, it could eventually lead to possession.

VIOLATING GOD'S LAW

In Deuteronomy 7:26 it talks about if you have one of these objects in your home what can happen. "Neither shalt thou bring an abomination into thine house, lest thou be a cursed thing like it: but thou shalt utterly detest it, and thou shalt utterly abhor it; for it is a cursed thing." This scripture is telling us that if these objects are in your possession or in your home, it can curse your life. A lot of people in our culture have these items in there home via DVDs, CDs, books, jewelry, and other things without really knowing what the real influence is and how these occultic powers influence them.

Hosea 4:6 says, "My people are destroyed for a lack of knowledge...." So, what you don't know can hurt you, but the good news is that the blood of Jesus is more powerful than any curse, hex, symbol, spell, talisman, or amulet. The symbol of the cross represents the shed blood of Jesus, which not only will pay for any sin you could ever think about, but it even protects you from all the power of Satan. As a believer, you must learn to exercise that authority through reading God's Word, prayer, and fasting. Asking Jesus Christ to be your Lord and save you, that's the first step. Before I got saved, I was involved with the occult. I had made a vow to Satan and even had spells cast on me. I possessed all types of amulets and charms that really affected me from addiction to simple blindness of the truth of the Gospel of Jesus Christ. Once I received forgiveness from my sins and made Jesus my King through His shed blood, all those spells and curses were broken and for the first time in my life I could truly live free. It's so important to be aware of the things that are in your possession, because if you are not, they could possess or oppress you!

Chapter 12
THE THEOLOGY BEHIND ECOLOGY: WICCA AND THE MODERN PAGANISM MOVEMENT

EARTH HISTORY

Without a doubt, our culture now more than ever needs to be responsible and conscious of how we use our natural resources. With the rise in worldwide pollution, the increase of energy consumption, drastic changes in our weather patterns, and a depleting ozone layer, environmental awareness and responsibility simply can not be ignored. For generations now we've heard the warnings by many different groups about the consequences of our lack of action in the environmental arena, but now we are seeing such an increase in the environmental catastrophes that it has demanded the world's focus.

Back in the 70's, 80's, and early 90's, non-profit environmental groups popped up all across the nation like:

Earth Counsel, Earth Life, Green Peace, Green Cross International, Society for Environmental Action, Friends of the Earth, Rainforest Action, and others. More recently, the Environmental Movement has gained momentum in different ways. More than two-thirds of Americans consider themselves environmentalists. According to the Internal Revenue Service, there has been a 51% increase in environmental non-profit organizations this decade.[132] According to Robert Bullard, who directs the Environmental Justice Resource Center at Clarke Atlanta University, "The environmental justice movement is growing swiftly. It's already increased from 300 groups in 1992 to more than 1,000 in 2000. Although 2/3rds of Americans might consider themselves environmentalist, only 8% actually are a member of an environmental group. The National Wildlife Federation has reported 700,000 new online members in the past 3 years alone.[133]

While big environmental green movement groups peaked out in the 1990's, especially with the 20th Anniversary of Earth Day, the movement continues to gain strength in more of a grassroots type of change. One of the stealthiest segments of the environmental movement and the fastest growing within the movement is ecospiritual, or ecoreligous groups. "Green" politics has become very powerful as well.

In the 1970's, when the movement was gaining world recognition and attention, the Congress passed many bills into legislation that would improve and protect the

---

[132] Mark Clayton, "Grassroots and Local Environment Groups Growing Across the US," Christian Science Monitor, 25 March 2004.
[133] Mark Clayton, p.4

environment such as "The Wilderness Act," and "The Clean Water Act." The Environmental Protection Agency was also formed in 1970 to enforce some of the legislation that was being put into place. The United Nations has been holding conferences on "environment" and "development" for decades, but is now working with groups like "Earth Counsel" to set global policy for environmental protection and awareness. One such policy is called "The Earth Charter." The Earth Charter's commission was established in 1997 by the UN to mobilize and implement rapidly, this planet saving document and to help work on and discuss other globalization agenda items.

With international disasters and world population increasing like it has, the only way to gain any ground on an international issue like the environment is through an international effort. While it is obvious international action needs to be taken to change the global problems on any significant level, what are some of the dangers that the environmental movement brings with it? Who are some of today's leaders in this movement? What do they believe? How is "green" politics shaping international environmental policy? How do Paganism, Wiccanism and Witchcraft tie into the environment? What does the Bible say about the environmental movement? Can a Christian be an environmental activist? As I stated earlier, the fastest growing sections of the environmental movement are ecospiritual and ecoreligious.

In his book, <u>Earth in Balance</u>, former Vice President Al Gore was quoted as saying, "The prevailing ideology of belief in prehistoric Europe and much of the world was based on the worship of a single earth goddess, who was assumed to be the fount of all life and who radiated harmony among all living things… It seems obvious that a better understanding of a religious heritage preceding our own by so many thousands of years could offer us new insights into the nature of the human experience."[134]

To what religious heritage is the former President referring that predates Christianity? The prehistoric European earth worship Mr. Gore was talking about has surged in the past few decades along with the environmental movement. Two major groups that are based in earth and nature worship are Neopaganism and Pantheism.

NEOPAGANISM AND PANTHEISM

Between 1300 and 1700, over 9 million women and girls were burned to death for practicing nature-earth worship, but now in America, witches can practice freely. The IRS has granted tax exemption to the Church and School of Wicca, which is a renewal of old style Paganism. Neo-Paganism or The New Paganism is defined by Craig S. Hawkins in his new book as a "revival of the old gods and goddesses of pre-Christian pale pagan polytheistic nature religions, mythologies, and mystery cults, such as Celtic, Norse, Greek, Egyptian, Roman, and other traditions of the western world… Astaroth, Diana, Hectate, Cernunnos, Osiris, Pan, and others are being invoked anew."[135]

Wicca, also biblically defined as witchcraft, is another part of the Neo-Pagan religious movement, which is nature oriented. Followers of Wicca worship believe in invoking

---

[134] Al Gore, <u>Earth In Balance: Ecology and the Human Spirit</u>, (Plume Books, Reprint Edition, January 1993) p.273.
[135] Craig S. Hawkins, <u>Witchcraft: Exploring the World of Wicca</u>, (Baker Books, 1996).

deities such as Mother Goddess or Horned God. They believe the gods are immanent deities pervading all of nature. Mother Goddess is primary and the Horned God is secondary. All other spirits are manifestations of one Mother Goddess. They believe the three phases of the Goddess are associated with the three phases of the moon: waxing, full, and waning. They believe the Goddess is associated with the Earth and is invoked by a variety of names. Aphrodite, Astarte, Diana, Cybele, Gaia, Isis, Vanus, and Luna are some of the names, but Diana is the most popular. Neo-Pagans believe that the Horned God is associated with the sun. They believe He is lord of the animals, death, and the afterlife. They believe that he dies every winter and is reborn every summer. They also believe that he is invoked by a variety of names, such as Adonis, Ammon-Ra, Osiris, Thor, and Pan. Pan is the most popular name in Witchcraft for the Horned God.

People that practice Witchcraft also practice Astrology and different forms of divination, special rites for seasonal holidays, and they practice magic spells and incantations using a pentacle as a symbol of the earth and the four elements as points in which they invoke deities. The inverted pentacle is a symbol of the Horned God Pan and is also a symbol of Satanists. Witches identify themselves as Pagans and nature worshipers. Terminology as earth or nature religion is commonly associated with most witchcraft groups. Margot Adler, author of <u>Drawing Down the Moon,</u> an exhaustive study on witches in America, said, "The resurgence of neopagan witchcraft is partially traceable to the environmental movement. It is partly a response to a planet in crisis; people today are looking for a religion that ties in with the natural world." [136]

Another teaching that is involved in these ecoreligious, ecospiritual parts of the environmental movement is based on Pantheism. Pantheism is the belief that God, or a group of gods, is identical with the whole natural world. Pantheism comes from Greek roots meaning "belief that everything is a god."[137] Most of Witchcraft, Buddhism, Hinduism, New Age, and Earth based religions fall into this category. Paul Harrison, a Pantheist, wrote a book called, <u>Elements of Pantheism: Religious Reverence of Nature and the Universe.</u> In this book, he gives us much insight into what exactly a Pantheist believes. He says, "Pantheism deeply reveres the universe and nature and joyfully accepts and embraces life, the body and earth, but does not believe in any supernatural deities, entities, or powers... When Pantheist say we revere and care for nature, we mean it with just as much commitment and reverence as believers speaking about their church or mosque, or the relics of their saints... Nature is the only place where we can find and make our paradise, not in some imaginary world on the other side of the grave. If nature is the only paradise, then separation from nature is the only hell. When we destroy nature, we create hell on earth." Mr. Harrison goes on to say "In this situation it (Pantheism) is becoming impossible to believe in gods other than the Universe itself, or gods who created this ungraspable immensity just as a frame for our tiny presence... In this generation spirituality must

---

[136] Margot Adler, <u>Drawing Down the Moon: Witches, Druids, and Goddess Worship,</u> (Beacon Press, March 1987) p.309.
[137] <u>Webster's New Riverside Desk Dictionary,</u> "Pantheism", (New York: Houghton Mifflin Company, 1988) p.306.

come of age and be reborn into the age of space, the age of science, and the age of environment."[138]

So basically, Neo-paganism is earth and nature based worship with the belief in invoking deities and Pantheism is earth and nature based worship that doesn't "invoke" deities, but say God is in all and all is in God and you are a god.

Just how far have teachings like Pantheism and Paganism gone on the realm of politics, education, and even religion? Who are the people leading this ecospiritual environmental revival?

Maurice Strong, the founder and leader of the Earth Counsel, is a senior advisor to the United Nations Secretary General of Kofi Anan. Strong has led the UN Environmental programs and conferences since the 1970's. In the early to mid-90's he and Mikhail Gorbachev, the president of Green Cross Int'l, launched an initiative called "Earth Charter." Strong owns a 200,000-acre New Age Zen colony in Colorado.[139] The Earth Charter topics were discussed in a 2002 World Summit with titles such as "Ethnical and Spiritual Challenges." The Earth Charter has reverence for Earth and the Cosmos as its core principle, but behind the Charter is a very clear paganistic agenda. While we must not ignore environmental issues, but rather be proactive, we must be able to separate the need to protect and preserve the Earth and its resources with paganistic/pantheistic views and concepts that have become

---

[138] Paul A. Harrison, Elements of Pantheism: The Religious Reverence of Nature and the Universe, (Lluina Press, Second Edition, May 1999) p.146.
[139] "An Interview with Ezra Levant, Author of Fight Kyoto," personal interview by Jim Fisher, Cat Country Radio, 9 December 2002.

so deeply embedded in the environmental movements groups.

ADAM AND EVE - ENVIRONMENTAL ACTIVISTS?

One question I hear frequently is, "What does the Bible say about the environment? I mean, can you be a Christian and an environmentalist, as well?" Actually, Yes! In Genesis 1:27-28, God told Adam and Eve to be environmentalist. "So God created man in his own image, in the image of God created he him; male and female created he them. And God blessed them and God said unto them, Be fruitful, and multiply, and replenish the earth, and subdue it: and have dominion over the fish of the sea, and over the fowl of the air, And over every living thing that moveth upon the earth."

God commanded man to be environmentally proactive in our use and management of the earth's natural resources, but God destroyed Pagan nations for worshipping earth and nature. God never intended for the people of the earth to worship nature.

Romans 1:20-23 says, "For the invisible things of him from creation of the world are clearly seen, being understood by the things that are made, even his eternal power and Godhead; so that they are without excuse: Because that, when they knew God, they glorified him not as God, neither were thankful; but became vain in their imaginations and their foolish heart was darkened. Professing themselves to be wise, they became fools, and changed the glory of the incorruptible God into an image made like to corruptible man, and to birds, and four footed beasts, and creeping things."

God created such an awesome creation (the earth, the sun, the moon) to glorify and prove the power of His existence. You can't look at our universe and deny the existence of God. But, what happened is that man, through Paganism and Pantheism started to worship creation instead of the Creator. That's like me walking up to a computer and saying "Wow, you're really smart! Computer, how did you create yourself? How did you design your software?" Someone much smarter than the computer designed it and then set it in motion. There is a push in the public schools of America to teach a curriculum called, "Intelligent Design". It basically teaches that the Universe is so complex that there must be a Divine being that designed it. Intelligent Design opens a door to tell about the biblical creation account of the Earth.

Hear is another question you might hear, "I thought it was okay to worship nature and God because He is all the same. What do I do?"

God wants you to respect and take care of the environment, but not worship it. That's idolatry and a form of witchcraft, which according to the Bible is an abomination in God's eyes. Make no mistake about it, God is much more than the environment. Step one would be to ask God to forgive your misunderstanding and sin, and apply the blood of Jesus over it. Understand the biblical plan God has for the Earth. Be responsible and take care of the Earth now and look forward to a new Heaven and new Earth in the re-generation. It will be here sooner than we think!

Chapter 13
THE ART OF MEDITATION: UNCOVERING TM

ACQUIRING THE FACTS

There are many forms of meditation practiced in America today. Everything from Hindu, Chi, Buddhist, Yoga, Taoist, Zen, to Transcendental Meditation are prevalent. Transcendental Meditation is the fastest growing form of meditation that there is presently. There are many similarities in the methods, forms, and chants of Buddhists, Yogas, Hindus, Zens, and Transcendental Meditationists. TM or Transcendental Meditation advocates are careful to point out that TM is not a religion and can be learned by and to benefit people of all cultures and religions.

America was mass introduced to TM in the 60's by its founder, Marharishi Mahesh Yogi, when he publicly associated himself and TM with the popular Rock-n-Roll band "The Beatles." Now, five generations later, TM has found its way into our society in many different forms and through many different avenues. Over 600,000 Americans claim to be TMs with 15,000 new enrollees every month. This makes TM one of the fastest growing movements numerically and financially. TM has found its way into local, state, and national governments all over the world. You can find the teachings of TM in all types of public institutions such as jails, hospitals, the armed services, and even America's public high schools.[140]

TM isn't free. As a matter of fact, TM is big business. TM is a non-profit educational organization, which is estimated to be valued at between $2 and $3 billion dollars. TM has initiation fees, which start from $125.00 to $1,000.00 followed by ceremonial processes, which can easily cost a pursuer of TM over $10,000 a year.[141] TM teachings and organizational titles are as follows: Students Int'l Meditation Society (SIMS), American Foundation for the Science of Creative Intelligence (AFSCI), Spiritual Regeneration Movement (SRM), International Meditation Society (IMS), Maharishi International University (MIU), and World Plan Executive Council (WPEC).[142]

A California state funded program called, "California Task Force to Promote Self Esteem" under the name "A World Safe for Children" teaches and promotes TM. In 1983, the U.S. Department of Education made a $250,000 grant to the Maharishi International University in Fairfield,

---

[140] Fundamentals of Progress, a TM publication, 1975, p.54

[141] Mike Doughney, "An Overview: The Transcendental Meditation Program," TM-Ex newsletter, Spring, 1991.

[142] M.H. Reynolds, Jr., "Transcendental Meditation: Is It Right for You?" Foundation Magazine, (Fundamental Evangelistic Association) p.3

Iowa.[143] In March of 2005, TM was taught to a group of teenagers in Augusta, GA at an area high school.[144] No doubt about it, from seminars for educators, health professionals, business and governmental leaders, to housewives and school kids, TM has definitely made its way in all forms into our culture.

TM: SCIENTIFIC OR RELIGIOUS

What exactly is "Transcendental Meditation?" A recent newspaper article promoting TM as a medical alternative for treating high blood pressure, heart attacks, and kidney diseases described TM as "a state in the mind of minimal activity. It typically involves a comfortable posture and the repetition of a carefully formulated but meaningless mantra to help clear thoughts."[145] Just how meaningless are these mantras? From where did TM originate? Who teaches the TM courses? What are some of the facts behind the Transcendental Meditation movement? TM, which claims to be scientific and not religious, was founded by Maharishi Mahesh Yogi. Maharishi was a 13 ½ year disciple of Swani Brahmananda Saraswati, one of the four major religious leaders of India.

THE ASCENT TO FAME

Maharishi was commissioned by his "ascended master" to evolve a simple form of meditation. He spent 2 years in seclusion in the Himalayas before he exported his teachings to England and America. A few years later the band called

---

[143] M.H. Reynolds, Jr., p.3

[144] Kelly Davis, "Transcendental Meditation: Ancient Indian Tradition Could Save Lives," <u>Anderson Independent</u> 19 March 2005: Life Section.

[145] Kelly Davis, Life Section.

"The Beatles" became converts and thus TM exploded in popularity in America.[146]

Maharishi is also well known for being a Yoga guru. Advocates of TM say the mantras are carefully formulated, but meaningless to help you clear your thoughts. At the very beginning of the TM program is the initiation ceremony in which the new coming candidate is given his own secret mantra. The "Sanskrit" or mantra given was to be meditated upon after the first ceremony. The initial ceremony or "puja" consists of the new convert or candidate plus the teacher going into an incense filled room; standing, or kneeling before a candlelit picture of the Guru Dev (divine teacher); and making a symbolic offering of 3 pieces of fresh sweet fruit, 6-12 fresh flowers and a new, white handkerchief, all of which must be brought by the candidate. The flowers represent life, the fruit represent the seed of life, and the white handkerchief represents the cleansing of the spirit. After the ceremony, there is a period of chanting, which includes many names of masters who have kept this technique intact for 1000's of years. Then, the instructor will turn to the candidate and ask them to repeat the "mantra," which is usually one or two syllable word.[147]

But are those mantras meaningless words to just clear your thoughts? Actually, the highly secret "mantras" given are names associated with Hindu deities. Maharishi said, "We select only mantras of personal gods... mantras fetch to us the grace of the personal gods." [148]The mantras are

---

[146] M.H. Reynolds, Jr., Life Section p.2.
[147] M.H. Reynolds, Jr., Life Section p.2.
[148] Mike Doughney, Spring 1991.

given based upon age, and/or sex of the person. A psychological definition of this process is called, "hypnotic trance induction." TM is not taught in books, but rather, only through teachers. Each teacher keeps the ceremony process secret and gives out the mantra, which their teachers instruct them to give out. Some of the mantras have been proven to be Krishna, Sarasvati, Shiva, and Kali to name just a few. The TM movement has claimed to have many mental and physical health benefits such as: reduced high blood pressure, reduced insomnia, reduced stress, increased energy, and increased overall health. They also claim that they have many findings that support these statements. But are these alternative health treatments effective and what is the process?

According to the Ayurveda, which is the Indian scriptures that TM is based on, you would treat alcoholism, anorexia, nausea, and poor digestion by taking goat feces washed with urine.[149] To treat inflammation, you would practice bloodletting.[150] To treat epilepsy, insanity, or seizures, you would drink donkey urine.[151] These are just a few examples. We don't know how effective these treatments really are, but we do know many studies found that half of the people who practice TM develop adverse affects.

We've already talked about the strong religious Hindu background of the founder Maharishi Mahesh Yoga, which means "Great Seer." "Although TM publicly denies its religious nature, the US Court of Appeals declared TM to

---

[149] Caraka Samhita, P.V. Editor-Translator, <u>Ayurvedic</u>, (Varanassi, India) vol.1, p.220.
[150] Caraka Samhita, p.220.
[151] Caraka Samhita, p.220.

be a religion, not suitable for public schools. The original TM incorporation in the US was used as a religious corporation. [152]

Maharishi teaches that God will not listen to your prayers without TM. These chants have been proven to be calling upon Hindu deities, which come from the Vedic Shankaracharya tradition writing, which are Hindu scriptures. In Psychology Today (April 1974), and article was written on TM which said, "The Science of Creation Intelligence (another name for TM) is clearly a revival of ancient Indian Brahmanism and Hinduism. Its origins lie in the Ancient text-Vedas, Upanishads Bhagavad-Gita, the teachings of Buddha and the synthesis of these traditions by Shankara. It has been simplified for modern Western consumption."[153] The Maharishi has been quoted as saying, "TM is a path to God."[154] He also said, "The Lord Krishna declares that realization of the state of all knowledge is the only way to salvation and success in life: there is no other way."[155]

A DOORWAY TO THE OCCULT

It is very clear that TM is a religion from the founder's statements and the facts that we looked at as well. What are some of the dangers of the TM program? It is very clear that TM, which embraces all religions, is a doorway to the occult. Some of the top websites on witchcraft have stated that meditation is one of the key steps in being involved in witchcraft. I, personally, knew people who practiced Astral

---

[152] M.H. Reynolds, p.2.
[153] M.H. Reynolds, p.2.
[154] Maharishi Mahesh Yogi, Meditations of Maharishi Mahesh Yogi p.59.
[155] Maharishi Mahesh Yogi, On the Bhagauad-Gita p.228.

Projection. Meditation was the entry door into this spiritual realm. Astral Projection is when someone, through occultic methods, leaves his body, and goes into the spirit world to travel to certain places after a period of meditation. They call this the astral. People who "channel spirits" practice "automatic writing," "levitation," or "the art of invisibility," do so through the door of meditation.

People, who practice "automatic writing", start by meditation. Automatic writing is when a person invites a demon into his body for demonic inspiration. Without a doubt, meditation is *a,* if not *the,* fundamental element in all occultic practices. The German government did studies on TM and found that, "TM results in tiredness, anxiety, depression, regression, suicidal tendencies, headaches, sleeping difficulties, neck pain, and twitching. These German government studies found that the teachers of TM were not qualified to deal with the problems associated with its practice."[156] The World Cult Awareness Network, The Task Force of Missionaries and Cults, and many other professional organizations have issued other warnings about the dangers of TM.

NONE OTHER NAME GIVEN

Over the years, I've had Christians ask me, "What does the Bible say about TM? Is it okay for a Christian to practice any form of meditation?" While TM isn't specifically mentioned in the Bible, we are able to look at the statements made by Maharishi and compare these statements with the scriptures. The Maharishi says, "The

---

[156] Leon S. Otis, <u>Adverse Effects of Transcendental Meditation</u> (Alden Publications, 1984) p.204.

true spirit of religion is lacking when it counts only what is right and wrong and creates a fear of punishment and hell and the fear of God in the mind of man."[157] The Bible says, "The fear of God is the beginning of wisdom." It also says in Matthew 10:28 (KJV) "And fear not them which kill the body, but are not able to kill the soul: but rather fear Him which is able to destroy both soul and body in Hell." The Maharishi says, "It does not matter whether they call themselves Christian, Mohammedan, Hindu, or Buddhist-any name will be significant."[158]

The Bible says in Acts 4:12, "Neither is there salvation in any other: for there is none other name under heaven given among men, whereby we must be saved." The Maharishi says, "I don't think Christ ever suffered or Christ ever could suffer."[159] The Bible says in I Peter 3:18, "For Christ also hath once suffered for sins, the just for the unjust, that He might bring us to God....."

Bible teaching clearly contradicts the concepts of TM. The Bible clearly teaches against the concepts of The Maharishi and warns us against such practices. TM calls upon Hindu gods in the chants they say and are based upon the Hindu Vedic, which are pagan teachings. Behind the very heart of TM is a Pagan based thinking repackaged and refurbished for an unsuspecting consumer.

Even though a U.S. Court of Appeals has deemed TM a religion, somehow its teachings have still slipped through the governmental boundaries laid out in our laws.

---

[157] Maharishi Mahesh Yogi, The Science of Being and Art of Living, TM publication, p.251.
[158] Maharishi Mahesh Yogi, The Science of Being and Art of Living, p.254.
[159] Maharishi Mahesh Yogi, Meditations of Maharishi Mahesh Yogi, p.123.

IS MEDITATING OKAY?

To answer the question, "Is it okay for a Christian to practice any form of meditation?" Yes, but it is not the kind of meditation that we have been talking about! The Bible says in the Psalm 19:14 to "Let the words of my mouth, and the meditation of my heart, be acceptable in thy sight, O Lord, my strength, and my redeemer." All throughout scripture, Christians are compelled by the writers to meditate on the teachings of Christ and the Holy Scriptures. During the process of meditation, a spiritual internalization of the concepts being taught takes place within your soul. However, unlike other forms of meditation, which call for an emptying of the mind, the Bible calls the believer to fill the mind with the truths of Jesus Christ and invite the Holy Spirit of Jesus Christ into the meditation process. Meditating on the blood of Jesus and the victory that the Atonement brings can cause a flood of the Holy Spirit to break forth into the believer's life. Learning to practice Christian meditation is essential for every believer.

Chapter 14
BEHIND THE CELEBRATION OF HALLOWEEN

IS IT A TRICK-OR-TREAT?

Halloween has become America's second largest celebrated holiday of the year, only second to Christmas. The average American family will spend $44.00 a child on Halloween. America will spend $586 million on decorations, $2 billion on candy, $1.5 billion on adult costumes, and $2.7 million on greeting cards, pumpkins, and party supplies for a total retail sale of $7 billion during Halloween. "Other holidays have become less important. Halloween is the exception. It has become more important," said Howard Davidowitz, expert on retail sales and president of a retail firm.[160] It seems that Halloween has become big business in the American retail market, but

---

[160] John Chartier, "Retailer's Not Spooked by Halloween," <u>Money</u>, (CNN, 21 October 2002) p.1.

what about the origins of Halloween? I mean, where did it all come from and what is it really all about?

It seems Halloween traditions, like many American holidays have been passed down from generation to generation from our dads and granddads and has sort of evolved each year taking on new additions and a few alterations. Over time, much of the original meaning has gotten somewhat distorted, so much to the point that no one really knows or pays attention to the core message.

With children all over the nation "trick-or-treating," dressing up in costumes, bobbing for apples, carving "Jack-o-Lanterns" out of pumpkins, having large parties, lighting big bonfires, and telling scary stories, it is a time when most American families have a great time together. For adults, it is a time when the biggest parties of the year are held and everyone flocks to the scariest haunted houses for thrills. All the scariest movies are released during Halloween. I can remember my earliest memory of Halloween. The first release of the movie "Halloween" had just come out and I watched it at a preacher's house. Then, we all went to a haunted house at the church later that night. I was so scared that I never wanted to go back there. With the recent increase of movies like the Harry Potter series, Van Helsing and other similar movies, we tend to lose sight of and sometimes shrug off the core message and meaning coming from these movies. It's the same with the Halloween celebration. The American culture has become desensitized to the real message of Halloween. When you think of Halloween, what do you think of? Most people are excited about the parties and the candy. Most people plan to attend Halloween parties or go trick-or-treating. It is time of fun!

But what are we excited about? What are we really celebrating?

Just think about a bunch of scary fantasies and stories with monsters and ghosts, witches and warlocks, tombstones and blood. Trick or treat? Blessing or curse? Where did it all come from and what does it all mean? Is it a bunch of silly stories and meaningless traditions or is there some truth and reality behind the traditions of the Halloween celebrations?

DISCOVERING THE ORIGINS

The word "Halloween" in the American Heritage Dictionary[161] says, "Halloween- October 31st, celebrated by children wearing costumes and begging for treats." Halloween's origins were not in America. America's version of the Halloween celebration came from "Samhain," an ancient Druidic fire festival celebrated by Celts who lived 2,000 years ago in the area that is now Ireland, the United Kingdom, and Northern France. They celebrated their New Year on November 1st.

Celts believed that on the night before the New Year on October 31st, the door between the worlds of the living and the dead became open. They believed that the ghosts of the dead returned to the earth. They believed that the evil spirits caused trouble and destroyed crops. They also believed October 31st was a time when their Druid priests could make predictions about the future by consulting the dead, much like the modern day psychics do. To celebrate the festival, the Druids built huge sacred bonfires, were Celts

---

[161] <u>American Heritage Dictionary</u>, (New York, NY: Dell Printing, 1994) p.378

gathered together to burn crops and offer animals as sacrifices to the Celtic deities, Gwynn Ap Nudd for the British and Arawn for the Welsh. During the bonfire festival, the Celts wore costumes and sat around the fire attempting to tell each other's fortunes. By 43 AD the Romans had conquered most of the Celtic territory. In the course of the 400 years the Romans ruled the Celtic lands, two Roman festivals were combined with the Druid festival of "Samhain." The first was Feralia, a day in late October when the Romans celebrated the passing of the dead and the second was the day of Pomona. Pomona was the Roman goddess of fruit and trees and her symbol was the apple.[162]

How did Halloween become the celebration that it is today? The Roman Catholic Church had a celebration called "All Saints Day," originally celebrated in May. This was a celebration to honor dead saints and martyrs. In 608 AD Roman Emperor Constantine pushed for the combination of the "All Saints Day," with the ritual of "Samhain." Some believe he was trying to appease the populace of new conquered territories. Pope Boniface IV moved it to November 1st. Rome's Pantheon, a temple built to worship a variety of gods was converted into a church. While Christians celebrated the death of saints on November1st, Pagans devoted the night before October 31st to the lord of the dead. Over the centuries, the night of "Samhain" and "All Saints Day" have been intertwined creating the American version of Halloween.[163] This is how Halloween originated! You can clearly see the origin of

---

[162] Chuck Missler, Signs in the Heavens, the Mysteries of the Planet Mars Halloween: Invitation to the Occult? (Kiononia House, 1991).

[163] Bob Larson, Satanism: The Seduction of America's Youth (Nashville, TN.: Thomas Nelson, Inc., 1989) p.40.

some things we do during this time like "bobbing for apples," carving pumpkins, and "trick-or-treating."

Here are some facts about Halloween other than just its history. October 31st, Samhain or Halloween is one of the four major holidays (called Sabbats), which Wiccans and Satanists observe.[164] Halloween costumes and bonfires on October 31st come from the ancient Druid ceremony of Samhain, where blood sacrifices were given to Celtic gods.[165]

The "Jack-o-Lantern" originated from occultists who would carve a scary face in a pumpkin and light a candle in it on their doorsteps on October 31st to scare away evil spirits that were released on this day of the dead. The practice of "bobbing for apples" brings together two Pagan traditions: divination and a fertility ritual. In some witchcraft covens, the closing ritual include eating an apple and/or engaging in fertility rites. The Roman goddess for fruit and trees is called "Pomona" and her symbol is an apple.[166]

The term "trick-or-treat" came from the Irish tradition when a man led a procession to ask for money from farmers. If the farmers would not, their crops would be cursed by demons. Black cats have represented, in the occult, incarnated humans, male violent spirits, or the "familiars" of witches.[167]

October 31st, 1517 was also the date Martin Luther nailed his 95 theses to a church door in Wittenberg, Germany, which started the protestant reformation. Perhaps

---

[164] Bob Larson, p.209.
[165] Bob Larson, p.42.
[166] Bob Larson, p.209.
[167] Bob Larson, p.42.

you are saying, "I understand the history is not godly, but how harmful can Halloween be? I'm not a witch or Satanist, I'm actually a Christian. I'm just trying to have a little fun! How harmful can Halloween really be? I mean, just because this stuff came from evil beginnings doesn't mean it's bad for me, is it?" We've already talked about the occultic beginnings of Halloween, but what does the Bible say about Halloween?

BLESSING OR CURSE?

Halloween is the day when divination is practiced around the world more than any other day of the year. Being a festival of the dead, it is a time when witches attempt to communicate with the dead in many different forms.

In Deuteronomy 18:9-13 NASB it says, "When you enter the land which the Lord your God gives you, you shall not learn to imitate the detestable things of those nations. There shall not be found among you anyone who makes his son or his daughter pass through the fire, one who uses divination, one who practices witchcraft, or one who interprets omens, or a sorcerer, or one who cast a spell, or a medium, or a spiritist, or one who calls up the dead. For whosoever does these things is detestable to the Lord; and because of these detestable things the Lord your God will drive them out before you. You shall be blameless before the Lord your God."

The Bible clearly tells us our festivals and celebrations are supposed to be focused on the Lord and the things concerning the kingdom of God. Our celebrations were never supposed to be focused on occultic history or their practices of the past. God gives clear warning about breaking this biblical law. God says to detest them, not celebrate them.

Because America has "learned to imitate" these detestable things in God's eyes, our whole society has taken on a heavy occultic influence and seductive bondage as a result of observing ungodly rituals, even as harmless as they seem. Hosea 4:6 says, "God's people are destroyed for a lack of knowledge." Ignoring God's law can hinder and even destroy your spiritual growth and walk with Jesus Christ. The effects of this can be seen in the youth of the Body of Christ. But can ignoring these laws and celebrating occultic holidays open a "door" spiritually? It is a scientific fact that the human brain is not finished developing until the average age of 21.

After talking to a child psychologist, she began to explain to me that during the first years 21 years of a person's life, their mind is still developing boundaries for morals. They are still deciding what is right and wrong. The younger the child is, the more impact the situations have on the development of that child's values. With America's glorification of the celebration of Halloween, especially with younger children, the effects on our culture's view of witchcraft and occultism can be very damaging. Many of the seemingly "harmless" Halloween traditions can be "entries" for the occult and can be very dangerous and destructive in the long run for the unaware, especially little children.

With the recent increase in occultic practices being glorified in our media, entertainment industry, board and card games, many Americans have been desensitized to the seriousness and dangers of occultism. The consequences of ignoring these seemingly harmless entry points can lead to serious demonic oppression and even possession.

Halloween is nothing more than an introduction to the occult. The scripture says in 2 Corinthians 6:15-18 "And what concord hath Christ with Be'lial? Or what part hath he that believeth with an infidel? And what agreement hath the temple of God with idols? For ye are the temple of the living God; as God hath said, I will dwell in them; and I will be their God, and they shall be my people. Wherefore come out from among them, and be ye separate, saith the Lord, and touch not the unclean thing and I will receive you, And will be a father unto you, and ye shall be my sons and daughters, saith the Lord Almighty." God clearly tells us to be separate from practices and celebrations like Halloween that have occultic origins. Even some practices in America's Easter and Christmas celebrations have been distorted over the centuries.

PROTECTING OURSELVES

Many people have asked me over the years, "What can we do to protect ourselves from these 'unknown' traps in our culture?" First, know the origins of Halloween. Recognize and define occultism biblically. Second, know that the only thing that can protect you completely from all demonic forces and can break every spell and hex is the blood of Jesus Christ over your life. The blood of Jesus is more powerful than any demon and not only that, but it completely washes your sins away.

Listen to this powerful description of the blood of Jesus, "For all have sinned and come short of the glory of God; being justified freely by his grace through the redemption that is in Christ Jesus, whom God hath set forth to be a propitiation through faith in his blood, to declare his righteousness for the remission of sins that are past, through the forbearance of God; To declare, I say at this time his righteousness that he might be just, and the justifier of him which believeth in Jesus"(Romans 3:23-26). This scripture says no matter what sin you've been involved in, occultism, pornography, murder, addictions, no matter what the sin, that the price of sin was paid for and the blood of Jesus broke the power of sin. It's the key ingredient to breaking beyond the darkness.

Chapter 15
OUT OF THE DARKNESS, INTO THE LIGHT

SURROUNDED BY DARKNESS

Have you ever had a moment in your life when you stopped, looked around and thought, "How in the world did I get here?" On August 16, 1998, I looked around and found myself starring into the eyes of leaders in the Church of Satan and the Santeria occult. It was exactly seven years to the hour from the night I made a vow to Satan on Jax beach in Florida. Here I was surrounded by darkness and for the first time in that seven-year period I could see what my life had become and where it was going.

Soon after that night on Jax beach in 1991, I became very ambitious selling drugs. I moved in with a group that was involved in Wicca and the New Age movement. I was selling drugs to everybody I could. Some of the people were heavily involved in witchcraft. Some were into the Mexican and Dixie Mafia; others in the Hell's Angels and some were in bands, such as 311 and Widespread Panic.

During these years of darkness, I experienced some very crazy things as I became closer to some of these people involved in witchcraft. I went from living on the streets of Atlanta, GA, to opening a bar in South Carolina. When I was in Atlanta, I went to all the music festivals, raves and clubs to sell drugs at the events. I was mentored in the bar business by a Reverend in the Church of Satan and a High Priest in the Santeria occult. These people took me in and where grooming me for this underground network they control. I can remember times when they would do rituals in the bar and release incantations (spells) over their bar and other businesses to be successful. I experienced two of my roommates becoming demonically possessed and questioning me on my views of sin. While living with them in a warehouse, the demonic oppression was so strong that, while under the influence of cocaine, I actually drank my own blood, and I did so without really knowing why I was doing it.

After five years of living this lifestyle, my brother asked me to help him establish a bar and grill in South Carolina. I wasn't exactly thrilled about leaving the fast-paced lifestyle of Atlanta, but I knew that I needed some change. Before I left, the Santeria priest released many incantations through spells, stones, herbs, and tarot cards over me, my brother, and the business we were about to open. For the next two years of my life, the bar and grill prospered, and so did the drug business. In the middle of all this success that I had longed for as a teenager came a very high price to pay. I had become very paranoid, greedy, and a miserable drug addict. I started snorting and shooting cocaine, and eating as many hits of ecstasy or acid as I could without overdosing. I did that on many occasions, and then I started to flirt with and even attempt suicide.

The more destructive and violent my behavior became, the greater my desire to become a member of this "elite" occultic network. I realized that my ties to these people stemmed from that night on the beach in Florida. During this time, a demon spirit started revealing himself to me. The spirit began tempting me with ideas about ruling the underworld and the business through its demonic power.

GETTING IN OR GETTING OUT

Around the same time, there were two very significant things that happened to me that caused me to question this dark path I had chosen. The first was one weekend I went up to the north Georgia mountains with an older leader in the Dixie Moffia to visit a trucking company they owned. They used this company as a front to transport drugs and launder money. Throughout the entire weekend, he kept giving me the introduction to his group trying to get me to work through them selling drugs. At the end of the weekend, one of his protégés took me outside during the day to show me something. As I stepped outside, this guy said something and extended his hand outward. Suddenly a blue lightning energy came shooting out of his fingertips. At this point, I began to understand just how serious my situation had become. During this same time, my business mentor from the church of Satan kept showing me his red card and asking me if I was interested in becoming an ordained minister! The pressure was unbelievable and the temptation was peaking. I knew something had to give. Either I was getting in or I was getting out, and it felt like in.

THE OFFER

On my 25th birthday, seven years to the night of my vow on the beach in Florida, I drove to Atlanta, GA to surprise my friends and celebrate my birthday. I was the one in for the big surprise on this particular night. When I arrived at the club, one of the largest rave clubs in Atlanta, all of my friends in this network were in the back office waiting for me. I told no one that I was traveling out of the state that night. Friends from all over the country 'just happened' to be there that night.

Toward the end of the night my mentor walked me up into the disc jockey's booth to show me something. He pointed over the sea of people dancing and asked me to look at their new "art work." As I looked over the crowd, I saw a painting of a dark angel with its wings spread, and in the corner I saw a dark perverted outline of Jesus. Nobody else could see the painting unless they were standing in the booth. The dark Reverend turned around, looked me in the eyes, and with his arms wide open, made me an offer of partnership in his business and an opportunity to be a brother in this network.

At that very moment, he turned around with his arms wide open and looked me in the eyes. A voice spoke to me and said, "Heaven is real, Hell is real, and you have to make a choice." Suddenly light filled every fiber of my body. I became completely conscious of my spiritual state. The drugs and alcohol seemed to fade away and the conviction from the Holy Spirit was the only thing on my mind. At that very moment, I made a new vow, this time to God. I prayed that if God would get me out of this situation, I would serve Him for the rest of my life. I spent the rest of the night listening to my mentor telling me his master plan of how we were going to become millionaires within six months to a year, but all I could think about was getting back to South Carolina and finding that old Bible that I had packed away years ago.

A NEW START

In the middle of the darkest time of my life, the light of Jesus Christ shone through every satanic curse and stronghold in my life in an instant. I Peter 2:9 says, "But ye are a chosen generation, a royal priesthood, an holy nation, a peculiar people; that ye should shew forth the praises of him who hath called you out of darkness into his marvelous light."

It doesn't matter in what kind of darkness you have ever been involved, the light of Jesus Christ, through His shed blood, is more powerful. Our culture has many avenues in which occultic doors can be opened in your life, but no demon spirit is more powerful than the blood of Jesus and the Holy Spirit of Jesus Christ, which lives in you after salvation.

That night, I left the rave club with my mentor and the other people there, who were involved in this occultic network. They took me to a warehouse downtown. As we pulled up, there was a hatch door that led to the basement. The basement was constructed of bricks and located in the center was one large room surrounded by doors leading into other rooms. On the walls in the center room were satanic symbols and writings in red. No one left the center room. My mentor stayed with me in the building telling me the details of his plan for the future. I was very scared, but I tried not to show any signs of fear.

Everybody in this room was involved in this network except the one friend I invited to come with us right before I left the club. I could tell my mentor was a little reluctant for my friend to come, but I knew that a blood sacrifice, or a ritual was the next step to do. During the course of the night my friend and I were able to quickly slip out of the warehouse and leave the downtown area.

I drove back to South Carolina the next day and for the first time in years my mind was clear and I could think clearly. I could hear and understand every demonic lyric to every song on my compact discs. I never recognized them before, but the Spirit of God, who is light, shined light into the dark areas of my life.

I started to read my Bible every time temptation would come to my mind. I was completely delivered from drug addiction, occultic spells, sexual perversion, violence, anger, greed, and much more through the blood of Jesus, praying and fasting, and quoting the written Word of God.

THE CALLING

God is calling a generation out of the darkness into His marvelous light. God is no respecter of persons. If God can make a way of escape out of the darkness for me, He will do it for anyone. I don't care how impossible a situation may seem, God's light will expose and expel any darkness in your life.

I began to fast and pray for this network of people in Atlanta. For six to nine months it was pure spiritual warfare in my life. People astral projected in my home, demons manifested to try to scare me and to stop my prayers, but I had light for the first time and no demon in hell could take that away from me. I was sealed with the Spirit of Light for eternity.

After about a year, I began to be mentored by Billy Mayo. He is the evangelist who had a similar conversion and exposed occultism in Rock music back in the late 80's and 90's through backward masking. This gave me a very powerful foundation to withstand darkness.

In 2002, God gave me a vision of a generation of young men and women who were being raised up to start a spiritual revolution in America. It was an Army of Light, a warrior nation that God was forming out of the Body of Christ to combat and conquer the darkness that has robbed multiple generations from their destiny.

October of that same year, my wife and I started "Warrior Nations International Ministries, Inc." It is a non-profit 501-C3 evangelistic outreach for the purpose of gathering in these men and women out of this dark culture and raising them up to be part of this warrior generation that is piercing and exposing the darkness of this American culture with the light of Jesus Christ.

We hold evangelistic meetings exposing cultural trends such as occultic music, movies, and much more, however the main purpose is to gather the harvest of souls into the Kingdom of God. We conduct meetings called, "Warring with the Word Conferences" that are designed to equip this army with the weapons they need to win this war on darkness. These conferences are an extension of our first book called, <u>Warring with the Word</u>.

There are many people and ministries God is raising up to fulfill this mandate, which is taking place in the spirit realm. There is a war cry going out in the spirit. It is a call to arms to battle this army of darkness with the unfailing power of the light of Jesus Christ.

God is calling an entire generation out of the dark pews of our churches, out of the dark alleys and the streets of America, out of the dark places of our culture, and into the marvelous army of light. Will you answer this call? Will you fight in this army of light? Will you help lead a generation out of darkness into their destinies? Will you be the one to answer the call and pierce beyond the darkness with the light of Jesus Christ?

Warrior Nations International Ministries, Inc. in Greenwood, South Carolina is the home of Shawn Patrick and Christy Williams' evangelistic outreaches. Shawn Patrick is also the Pastor of Faith Family Harvest Church and the host of the *Beyond the Darkness* television show.

To contact Shawn Patrick Williams write:
Warrior Nations International Ministries, Inc.
PO Box 2352
Greenwood, South Carolina 29646
864-227-0508

You may also e-mail Shawn Patrick from his website @ www.warriornations.org.

Warrior Nations International Ministries, Inc. in Greenwood, South Carolina is the home of Shawn Patrick and Christy Williams' evangelistic outreaches. Shawn Patrick is also the Pastor of Faith Family Harvest Church and the host of the *Beyond the Darkness* television show. To contact Shawn Patrick Williams write:

Warrior Nations International Ministries, Inc.
PO Box 2352
Greenwood, South Carolina 29646
864-227-0508
www.warriornations.org.

To order additional copies of this book or to see a complete list of all **ADVANTAGE BOOKS™** visit our online bookstore at:

www.advbookstore.com

or For Book Orders Only, call our toll free order number at:

1-888-383-3110

Longwood, Florida, USA

"we bring dreams to life"™
www.advbookstore.com

Printed in the United States
200319BV00008B/172-753/A

9 781597 551014